SUPPORTING

UNDERSERVED

STUDENTS

How to Make PBIS
Culturally & Linguistically Responsive

SHARROKY HOLLIE | DANIEL RUSSELL JR.

Solution Tree | Press

555 North Morton Street
Bloomington, IN 47404
800.733.6786 (toll free) / 812.336.7700
FAX: 812.336.7790

email: info@SolutionTree.com
SolutionTree.com

Visit **go.SolutionTree.com/diversityandequity** to download the free reproducibles in this book.

Printed in the United States of America

Library of Congress Cataloging-in-Publication Data

Names: Hollie, Sharroky, 1967- author.
Title: Supporting underserved students : how to make PBIS culturally and linguistically responsive / Sharroky Hollie, Daniel Russell Jr.
Other titles: How to make Positive Behavioral Interventions and Supports culturally and linguistically responsive
Description: Bloomington, IN : Solution Tree Press, [2021] | Includes bibliographical references and index.
Identifiers: LCCN 2021047290 (print) | LCCN 2021047291 (ebook) | ISBN 9781952812293 (Paperback) | ISBN 9781952812309 (eBook)
Subjects: LCSH: School discipline--United States. | Culturally relevant pedagogy--United States. | Children of minorities--Education--United States.
Classification: LCC LB3012.2 .H65 2021 (print) | LCC LB3012.2 (ebook) | DDC 371.50973--dc23/eng/20211116
LC record available at https://lccn.loc.gov/2021047290
LC ebook record available at https://lccn.loc.gov/2021047291

Solution Tree
Jeffrey C. Jones, CEO
Edmund M. Ackerman, President

Solution Tree Press
President and Publisher: Douglas M. Rife
Associate Publisher: Sarah Payne-Mills
Art Director: Rian Anderson
Managing Production Editor: Kendra Slayton
Copy Chief: Jessi Finn
Senior Production Editor: Christine Hood
Content Development Specialist: Amy Rubenstein
Acquisitions Editor: Sarah Jubar
Copy Editor: Jessi Finn
Proofreader: Mark Hain
Text and Cover Designer: Abigail Bowen
Editorial Assistants: Charlotte Jones, Sarah Ludwig, and Elijah Oates

ACKNOWLEDGMENTS

This book was written during the COVID-19 pandemic and during the most intense moments of the racial justice reckoning. Educators stepped up to respond in both instances for their students like never before. I want to acknowledge the most incredible teachers and administrators that I had the honor of working with during an unprecedented time. Their steadfastness, flexibility, and resourcefulness served as inspiration for continuing to write when it seemed like our world was falling apart. Even though I was quarantined, as we all were, witnessing firsthand the diligence and perseverance of educators from Seattle to San Diego, from Lansing to Los Angeles, and from Miami to Milwaukee reminded me of the need for this text and its potential for impact.

I want to also acknowledge my family for tolerating my isolation while writing during our time of collective isolation and for allowing me the physical space in our crowded home that I could claim without worry of disruption. I am most grateful for your continued support, trust, and belief in my passion for supporting underserved students.

—Sharroky Hollie

I co-wrote this book with Sharroky while completing my doctoral dissertation at the University of Southern California's Rossier School of Education. Needless to say, the combination of authoring a book and earning my doctorate simultaneously was time consuming and required much time away from my loved ones. Therefore, I would be remiss in not acknowledging my wife and kids, as they too sacrificed quality family time in support of me accomplishing these concurrent goals. To my wife, I am thankful to you for taking on the extra load in parenting as I was immersed in my writing and for being a constant believer in my pursuit to address racial inequities in discipline. To my children, I am grateful for your understanding as I missed out on family vacations and some of your sporting events. You continued to support what I endeavored to achieve. I also want to thank my parents for instilling in me the meaning of hard work and standing up for what I believe in. I especially want to express my heartfelt thanks to my mother. Mom, you never had the opportunity for a formal education like I received, and you did not live to see me accomplish these goals, but you were my constant *why* throughout this process.

Besides my family, I also want to acknowledge all the others in my career in education who have contributed directly and indirectly to me finding my voice for this book.

First, to all the students whom I have had the honor and privilege to teach or work with—I thank you for making me a more responsive educator. Next, I would like to express my gratitude to all the colleagues, mentors, and educators I have had the opportunity to work with throughout my twenty-seven years in public school education. I have learned much with and from you. Last, I would like to say thanks to my professors at USC Rossier School of Education who steadfastly believed in me as a writer while also helping me grow as a writer.

—*Daniel Russell Jr.*

Solution Tree Press would like to thank the following reviewers:

Jessica Djabrayan Hannigan
Assistant Professor,
   Educational Leadership
California State University
Fresno, California

Ursala Maddox Davis
Coordinator of Teacher Effectiveness
Rockdale County Public Schools
Conyers, Georgia

Emily Terry
English Teacher
Kinard Middle School
Fort Collins, Colorado

Kaitlyn Zytkoskee
Fourth-Grade Teacher
Roy Elementary School
Eatonville, Washington

Visit **go.SolutionTree.com/diversityandequity** to download the free reproducibles in this book.

TABLE OF CONTENTS

FINAL THOUGHTS

APPENDIX

ABOUT THE AUTHORS

 **Sharroky Hollie, PhD,** is a national educator who provides professional development to thousands of educators in the area of cultural responsiveness. Since 2000, Dr. Hollie has trained more than 150,000 educators and worked in over 2,000 classrooms. Going back to 1992, he has been a classroom teacher at the middle and high school levels, a central office professional development coordinator in the Los Angeles Unified School District (LAUSD), a school founder and administrator, and a university professor in teacher education at California State University, Dominguez Hills. Dr. Hollie has also been a visiting professor for Webster University in St. Louis, Missouri, and a guest lecturer at Stanford University and the University of California, Los Angeles.

In addition to his experience in education, Dr. Hollie has authored several texts and journal articles. Most recently, he coauthored *Beyond Conversations About Race: A Guide for Discussions With Students, Teachers, and Communities* (2020), wrote *Strategies for Culturally and Linguistically Responsive Teaching and Learning* (2015), and contributed a chapter in *The Oxford Handbook of African American Language* (2015).

Dr. Hollie's first book, *Culturally and Linguistically Responsive Teaching and Learning: Classroom Practices for Student Success*, was published in 2011, followed soon thereafter by *The Will to Lead, the Skill to Teach: Transforming Schools at Every Level*, cowritten with Dr. Anthony Muhammad. In 2003, he and two colleagues founded the Culture and Language Academy of Success, a laboratory school that demonstrated the principles of cultural responsiveness in an exemplary schoolwide model, which operated until 2013. Dr. Hollie received his PhD from the University of Southern California in curriculum and instruction, with an emphasis on professional development, and his masters in English education from California State University, Northridge.

To learn more about Dr. Hollie's work, visit the Center for Culturally Responsive Teaching and Learning (www.culturallyresponsive.org) or follow him @validateaffirm on Twitter.

 **Daniel Russell Jr., EdD,** is the coordinator of research and development and a lead cultural and linguistic responsiveness (CLR) coach for the Center for Culturally Responsive Teaching and Learning. There, he leads training and professional development and provides one-on-one coaching in CLR. He particularly specializes in providing training on how to align positive behavioral interventions and supports (PBIS) with CLR. Additionally, he collects and analyzes data for the Center for Culturally Responsive Teaching and Learning, as well as curates resources for the center's CLR Responds to R.A.C.E. Challenge.

Dr. Russell, who entered teaching in the LAUSD in 1994 through Teach for America, is a former classroom teacher with twenty-one years of experience teaching both elementary and middle school. During his tenure as a teacher in the LAUSD, he also served as a teacher facilitator for the Academic English Mastery Program (AEMP), an English language coordinator, a specially designed academic instruction in English trainer, and an induction coach. He also worked as a corps member advisor at a Teach for America Summer Institute. Dr. Russell followed his years working in the LAUSD by being a founding teacher at Culture and Language Academy of Success (CLAS) with Dr. Sharroky Hollie. From there, he went on to work as a teacher and dean of students at a charter school in the Los Angeles area.

During his career as an educator, Dr. Russell received several recognitions. As an LAUSD intern, he was given the Golden Apple Award for being a distinguished intern. LAUSD's AEMP also honored him with the Outstanding AEMP Facilitator and Outstanding Teacher awards. In 2005, he and his class were featured on a segment of the PBS documentary *Do You Speak American?* The segment focused on African American language and what his students learned about linguistic codeswitching through AEMP. He is currently a member of the American Educational Research Association.

Dr. Russell received his bachelor's degree in U.S. history from San Diego State University in 1994, and he earned his National Board Certification for middle childhood, generalist, in 2001. He completed his final semester at the University of Southern California's Rossier School of Education in 2021, where he received his EdD in organizational change and leadership. His dissertation focused on the persistent overrepresentation of Black students in exclusionary discipline at schools implementing PBIS.

To book Dr. Sharroky Hollie or Dr. Daniel Russell Jr. for professional development, contact pd@SolutionTree.com.

The Ubiquity of Positive Behavioral Interventions and Supports

"UBIQUITY DOES NOT ALWAYS EQUAL SUCCESS"
SHARROKY HOLLIE

My dissertation chair and PhD program adviser was Dr. David Marsh, who, at the time, was a well-known and respected expert on educational systems reform, innovations, and implementation in relation to effective professional development. Because of Dr. Marsh, I had the good fortune of not only becoming aware of research giants like Michael Fullan and Thomas Guskey, but I was able to study their respective work deeply and critically. One of my lasting learnings from Dr. Marsh was looking at prolific or popular professional development programs or approaches in schools and their particular or potential impact as a school innovation.

I remember doing an assignment on Ruby Payne's A Framework for Understanding Poverty *(2019) which was, at one time, one of the most utilized professional learning opportunities in the United States (Bohn, 2006), even before it received noteworthy attention in terms of a research-studied practice that had been critically analyzed from the academic community in higher education. As of the writing of this book,* A Framework for Understanding Poverty, *now in its 6th edition, has sold more than 1.5 million copies. As Anita Bohn (2006) puts it, Payne's work has been the single-most influential voice on teachers' perspectives about students living in poverty in the past thirty years. Since 1996, Payne has conducted more than two hundred seminars each year, reaching over 25,000 educators every year. You do the mathematics. Bohn claims that* A Framework for Understanding Poverty *has been experienced in 70 percent of all U.S. school districts in some capacity.*

However, in a critical examination of Payne's framework, "Questioning Ruby Payne," Adrienne Van der Valk (2016) says, "The current evidence base for the Payne School Models, as provided in the reports and as reviewed here, simply cannot support confident causal claims about its effectiveness" (p. 4). Without getting into the controversies of Payne's work, my takeaway from this assignment was that in professional learning spaces, especially in education, ubiquity can overshadow the intended result of being effective and making significant differences for historically marginalized students. The point of this story is not to criticize Payne. From a research perspective, the message was that the ubiquity of an approach or program does not automatically equal overall effectiveness. Payne's A Framework for Understanding Poverty *(2019) is a good example of that dynamic. The central purpose of this book, however, is to increase the likelihood that positive behavioral interventions and supports, better known as PBIS, in its ubiquity will be effective for all students, especially the underserved. PBIS and schoolwide positive behavioral interventions and supports (SWPBIS) originated through the work of researchers George Sugai and Robert Horner (2002) at the University of Oregon, and almost twenty years later in 2021, it is now ubiquitous in 21st century schools.*

Since about 2012, very few schools that we support with cultural and linguistic responsiveness (CLR) do not use PBIS in some fashion. In short, PBIS is almost everywhere. We have educated and supported educators in becoming more culturally responsive through professional learning and through school-site, embedded support, which we will reference throughout the text (Hollie, 2018). In most of the districts we have worked, staff raise questions about widespread PBIS professional development and schoolwide PBIS implementation compared to its actual effectiveness, especially with students of color. Therefore, many educators ask us about PBIS's effectiveness in relation to cultural and linguistic responsiveness.

The Purpose of This Book

At the outset, let us be clear. This is not a book designed to criticize PBIS. We wrote this book to help districts realize their need to align PBIS with cultural responsiveness, thereby positively impacting the learning experiences of *all* students, and Black and Brown students specifically. But with this purpose comes an irony that is twofold.

The first irony is that although PBIS has a far reach from district to district, we have noticed that *culturally responsive teaching*, used here as just a generic term for the overall concept of responding to students in a way that meets their needs culturally and linguistically (Hollie, 2018), has little reach in many of those same districts (Russell, 2021). Many districts are hardly scratching the surface of being culturally responsive, while at the same time they are steeped in PBIS. When we look at the wealth of resources that come with PBIS (such as mandated districtwide professional development on PBIS, the infusion of PBIS into school behavioral support systems, and the creation of central office PBIS positions), we compare those resources with what districts are doing with cultural responsiveness. It is never a fair comparison. Meaning that, as it applies to cultural responsiveness, it rarely if ever is mandated, is not infused into school behavioral on instructional support systems, and central office positions intended for support of cultural responsiveness are few and far between. The unintended result is that the use of PBIS is ubiquitous across districts, while the districts have a dearth of culturally responsive teaching.

For example, before the COVID-19 pandemic, we were consulting with a district in the Midwest, and we were sent to the district's flagship school for PBIS. It was supposedly a model of high implementation, and the school leader and the teachers were very proud of their award banner on the wall. In our discussions about the school's high levels of PBIS implementation, the staff revealed that their discipline data showed African American students were still being disproportionately suspended and referred out of class in comparison to other student populations in their school. In fact, the rate of disproportionality had increased over the past year. After they presented this data point, the room became silent, which spoke loudly for what could not be said. Despite PBIS's success and prevalence in this school, it was still failing its students of color, which is the second irony.

Typically, during our work with cultural responsiveness with school districts, district representatives ask what they can do to align cultural responsiveness and PBIS. Our first response is always to find out more about their PBIS implementation and the specific related issues. We find that, for most districts, the main issue is the same—the students of color are referred out of class or suspended from school at rates that are not proportionate to their population in the said school or district. In one district we work in, African American students are only 5 percent of the student population, but they make up almost 25 percent of the suspensions. In education jargon, this is called *disproportionality*. As far as they are concerned, they are implementing PBIS successfully, yet discipline and disparity issues persist, especially with their Black and Brown students. With our support, these districts hope they can apply what they are learning about cultural responsiveness to their PBIS and close the disproportionality gap. After dozens and dozens of conversations with schools about this issue, it was clear there was a need for a structured and comprehensive alignment of PBIS to CLR, hence the creation of this book.

Because of PBIS's ubiquity, we understand the significance of aligning PBIS with cultural and linguistic responsiveness. We have seen the frustration in the eyes of too many district leaders, school-site administrators, PBIS coaches, and classroom teachers. On the one hand, they see PBIS working, but on the other hand, they also see it is not working for *all* students. With contrast comes a feeling that something is missing. Our hypothesis is that the missing piece is cultural and linguistic responsiveness. We have seen firsthand how when districts align their PBIS with cultural and linguistic responsiveness, it can have positive implications around student outcomes around classroom management and discipline. We have seen schools and districts expend large amounts of time, money, and energy, only to yield returns below what they expected. Most poignantly, we have seen dire results with many students, but especially for those who needed success more urgently or whom we call the underserved. We define *underserved* as any student, regardless of race or ethnicity, who is not having success academically, socially, or behaviorally because the school *is not being responsive to their cultural and linguistic needs* (Hollie, 2018).

The Contents of This Book

The book is divided into two parts, and each part has three chapters. Part 1 provides a rationale for *why* PBIS needs to be aligned to cultural and linguistic responsiveness. Chapter 1 establishes the basics of a CLR-managed classroom, which includes clarity on cultural and linguistic responsiveness as a specific concept and type of culturally responsive teaching. Chapter 2 answers the question, Is PBIS by nature culturally and linguistically responsive for all students? You can probably guess the answer, but this chapter provides the rationale and reasons for that answer. Then, chapter 3 lays out an argument for *authentic* alignment of CLR and PBIS, which gets at the heart of any potential disconnect between CLR and PBIS, and offers a realistic probability for coexistence.

Part 2 provides the *how* for aligning CLR and PBIS, using practical steps, suggestions, and recommendations. Chapter 4 shares three steps for starting the process: (1) alignment, (2) assessment, and (3) activation. Chapter 5 presents opportunities for creating situational appropriateness, the goal of CLR within the PBIS framework. Finally, chapter 6 shares language, activities, and procedures for fostering situational appropriateness in various school situations affected by PBIS. Each chapter features personal anecdotes and stories from the authors, which give special insight and life to the research. The end of the book offers an appendix with a list of helpful abbreviations related to PBIS and cultural and linguistic responsiveness.

Conclusion

It bears repeating. The purpose of this book is not to criticize PBIS. It is quite the opposite. Our intention is to *enhance* PBIS in a way that will increase its likelihood of success with underserved students, regardless of their background. Given PBIS's prevalence, we want it to have a positive impact for the students who need it the most. In effect, we hope to meet a demand and address a need.

How does PBIS look when it is implemented in a culturally and linguistically responsive way? From our knowledge, there is no other book or resource that tackles this question head on and does so unapologetically, while at the same time challenging if cultural and linguistic responsiveness has been infused with depth and fidelity, if at all. We offer a reflective process that comes with concrete examples, specific recommendations, and delineated procedures all throughout the text to engender a "no-excuse" opportunity for alignment of PBIS with CLR. We assume that our goal, albeit simple but ambitious, is the same as yours—successful and equitable outcomes for all students.

The *Why* of Culturally and Linguistically Responsive PBIS

At first glance, some might question why PBIS needs to be aligned with CLR. In most cases, it originated as a district mandate backed by federal law in regard to creating positive discipline support as opposed to punitive-based discipline practices. In addition, PBIS has been well-funded and supported, although not evenly implemented. All these factors create a sense of "if ain't broke, don't fix it."

The problem is that while PBIS worked for some, it was broken for others. As you will learn in part 1, even the creators and early implementers knew there was a need for PBIS to be aligned to cultural responsiveness. Therefore, the main reason PBIS needs to be aligned to CLR is because its originators said it boldly and courageously. Another is that in the schools and districts we have worked with, educators seem to be floundering with their PBIS and its perceived disconnect with cultural responsiveness. The first part of the book addresses these two needs directly.

Chapter 1 starts off with a discussion of what it means to be culturally and linguistically responsive, as defined by our research over twenty years, and what a culturally and linguistically managed classroom entails. Chapter 2 discusses knowing what it means to have culturally and linguistically responsive classroom management in the context of PBIS. More specifically, this chapter delves into the inherent philosophical differences that educators must understand in order to align the two. Understanding this difference allows for acknowledging the elephant in the room that sometimes remains between the lines in discussions about PBIS and CLR. Finally, chapter 3 gets to the crux of the need for alignment by focusing on the PBIS deficit orientation that is often missed. We provide examples of this orientation, as well as the impetus for the *how* of alignment, which follows in part 2.

CHAPTER 1

The Basics of a CLR-Managed Classroom

"STARTING A NEW SCHOOL"
SHARROKY HOLLIE

In 2003, Daniel and I, along with a team of colleagues, started a new school called the Culture and Language Academy of Success (CLAS). Endorsed by the Los Angeles Unified School District (LAUSD), CLAS was a preK–8 independent public charter school that existed for ten years (2003–2013). At its height, CLAS successfully served nearly four hundred students and their families each year (Orange & Hollie, 2014). Our student population was 99 percent African American, even though we were open for all students. CLAS was a laboratory school that applied cultural and linguistic responsiveness as a schoolwide philosophy and the basis of our instructional program. Our philosophy was based on meeting students where they were culturally and linguistically as the first teaching in all aspects, including how we managed our classrooms and how we disciplined students.

This school served as a national model for how to validate and affirm or be culturally responsive in general for all students, but in particular with African American students (Orange & Hollie, 2014). Visitors would come from all over the United States to see cultural and linguistic responsiveness in practice because during the early 2000s, there were very few models of what cultural and linguistic responsiveness looked like nationwide. I will never forget a comment from an administrator who was visiting from Northern California. She stated, with tears in her eyes, "I don't think I have seen this many Black kids so happy while at school."

To this day, starting a school from the ground up remains my most challenging and rewarding professional accomplishment by far. I liken it to caring for a newborn baby, in particular the middle-of-the-night feedings and frequent diaper changings—and I am speaking from experience as a parent.

Just like with newborns, I still remember, without much joy, that first school year at CLAS when I would wake up at 3:00 a.m. pretty much every day. During that first year, we had not found a morning care program that aligned with our culturally and linguistically responsive approach, and we could not afford a full-time custodian. So I had to open the school at 6:30 a.m. because in addition to being the morning care person, I had to sweep the wood chips left on the ground from the outdoor play apparatus from the previous day. The morning care programs we explored typically espoused a more traditional approach to classroom management and discipline, which did not have the same mindset as ours. Our focus and commitment to being culturally and linguistically responsive became our star on the map and a novelty in the landscape of public education at the time (Orange & Hollie, 2014). Visitors frequently asked, "What is your classroom management program or approach?" Over the years, we developed a stock answer in anticipation of the question, which explained the basics of a culturally responsive classroom management approach. This first chapter is the answer to that question.

The opening anecdote is not just a story for the sake of telling a story. Our experiences and research at CLAS will be an important theme throughout this text because it is at CLAS where we cut our teeth for what it means to align PBIS with CLR. The early learnings that began at CLAS led to the core tenets, principles, and strategies necessary for the alignment, therefore providing the best model, and to some extent evidence, for what we are presenting in this book. Therefore, we know that PBIS can be aligned to CLR successfully. The first chapter begins a deep exploration into the processes and practices you need to know, so the alignment of your PBIS with CLR can be successful.

Through our collaborative work at CLAS, we developed a culturally and linguistically responsive classroom management approach with which we were able to experiment over the tenure of the school (Hollie, 2018). We concluded that there are three integral steps to the approach:

1. Apply the core principles of CLR with authenticity.
2. Implement an effective classroom management system.
3. Determine what behaviors are cultural and what behaviors are not acceptable, with a commitment to validate and affirm the cultural behaviors.

The first step, applying the core principles of CLR with authenticity, defines CLR and what makes it different from other types or brands of cultural responsiveness; explains what it means to validate, affirm, and build and bridge (VABB); and describes how VABBing is linked to instruction and cultural and linguistic behaviors. The second step, implementing an effective classroom management system, discusses the practices necessary for any system to be successful, according to classroom management research. Then, we identify which classroom management systems are congruent with the principles of CLR. The third step, determining what behaviors are cultural and what behaviors are not acceptable, explores cultural behaviors that traditional schooling tends to misunderstand or misinterpret, which might be considered the root problem of misaligning PBIS with CLR. Note that this book will not provide an overview of the entire CLR approach, but only cover the integral components of CLR that are pertinent to a culturally responsive classroom management system (CRCM). For a full explanation of CLR as an approach, we recommend that you read Hollie (2018) or Muhammad and Hollie and (2012).

Apply the Core Principles of CLR With Authenticity

The first step to establishing a culturally responsive classroom management system is applying the core principles of CLR with authenticity, which we will explore in this first section. The core principles are as follows:

- Understand the definition of cultural and linguistic responsiveness.
- Identify your brand of cultural responsiveness.
- Know the meaning, purpose, and *how* of validating, affirming, building, and bridging.

First, we will define CLR and its essential purpose of validating, affirming, building, and bridging. We also briefly discuss what distinguishes CLR from other brands of culturally relevant teaching (Hollie, 2019a). Then we will explore the *how* of CLR, which is demonstrated through the CLR formula of success and focuses on specific cultural and linguistic behaviors.

Understand the Definition of Cultural and Linguistic Responsiveness

Based on twenty years of experience and research, we have cultivated the following definition of *cultural and linguistic responsiveness (CLR)*: "the validation and affirmation of the home (indigenous) culture and home language for the purposes of building and bridging the student to success in the culture of academia and mainstream society" (Hollie, 2018, p. 23). CLR is meeting students where they are culturally and linguistically for the purpose of bringing them where they need to be academically in the context of the school culture.

Another way of looking at CLR is to see it as the opposite of the sink-or-swim approach to schooling. CLR's approach is to support the struggling "swimmers" or students who cannot swim at all, meaning the students who don't do school well based on the cultural norms of traditional schooling. In other words, CLR supports the underserved students or those who are failing academically, socially, or behaviorally *because the school is not being responsive to who they are culturally and linguistically* (Hollie, 2018).

In *The Will to Lead and the Skill to Teach*, co-written with Anthony Muhammad (2012), Hollie proffers another way of looking at CLR by calling it "skilled pedagogy," or the *how* and *why* of teaching and the strategic use of methods and techniques, and a rationale behind why decisions are made instructionally to best serve the students who are most in need. The rationale is based on the essential core of CLR—validating and affirming cultural and linguistic behaviors and building and bridging to academic and social skills within the school context. First, it's important to distinguish CLR from other brands of cultural relevance, now that it has been defined.

Identify Your Brand of Cultural Responsiveness

We learned over the years that there are many different names for and interpretations of cultural relevance. In an article for *Teacher Education Quarterly*, Hollie (2019a) critically challenges an aspect of culturally relevant teaching, specifically how the terms *culturally relevant* and *culturally responsive* had become buzzwords, and therefore cliché. They had become so generic over time that they had lost their core meaning. Hollie (2019a) states:

> [Culturally relevant teaching] has to be more than just a name, and there are plenty of names to choose from when it comes to CRT. They include, among others, culturally responsive pedagogy, culturally compatible teaching . . . culturally connected teaching, culturally competent, culturally responsive learning, culturally matched teaching, cultural proficiency, culturally sensitive teaching, culturally proficient, cultural competency, culturally appropriate teaching, and now [culturally sustaining pedagogy]. (p. 37)

In the article, Hollie calls for a "branding" of the different types of cultural relevancies so people could recognize their distinct differences, giving them more significance as individual brands as opposed to one overall approach. The article includes a full survey of the different brands of culturally relevant teaching. Most relevant to this text, however, is that CLR is a specific brand to align with PBIS. *Culturally responsive teaching* is not used here in the generic sense. CLR as a brand is specifically rooted in the work of theorists Geneva Gay (2000) and Lisa Delpit (2006). Gay (2000) defines *culturally responsive pedagogy* as "the use of cultural knowledge, prior experiences, frames of reference, and performance styles of ethnically diverse students to make learning encounters more relevant to, and effective for them. This pedagogy teaches *to and through* the strengths of these students. It is culturally validating and affirming" (p. 31).

Our conceptualization of CLR keys in on two aspects of this definition. One is the focus on pedagogy. The attention to instruction impacted our perspective because we were able to align CLR with the research that shows instruction is the strongest variable linked to student achievement (Hattie, 2012). What matters the most is the *how* of the cultural responsiveness or pedagogy, not the *what*, meaning a focus on content. The second aspect of Gay's (2000) view is the last line of her definition. She states that culturally relevant pedagogy is *culturally validating and affirming*. From the very first time we read the work of Geneva Gay, those two words, *validating* and *affirming*, resonated. Our fundamental belief is that above all, pedagogy, the *how* of classroom teaching, should first and foremost authenticate and support students' cultural and linguistic backgrounds and behaviors. The philosophical underpinning of CLR is therefore rooted in a construct called *validate, affirm, build, and bridge* based originally on the work of Geneva Gay.

Know the Meaning, Purpose, and *How* of Validating, Affirming, Building, and Bridging

CLR revolves around four essential words—*validate, affirm, build*, and *bridge*. The following sections explore what these terms mean in the context of CLR, their purpose, and also, how to implement them in a culturally responsive classroom.

The Meaning

We describe *validation* as the intentional and purposeful legitimization of the home culture and language of the student. The delegitimization occurs through the mainstream and social media's stereotypes and generalizations, the historical deficit perspective of so-called research, and the documented inequities in social institutions. The commonality is that in one way or another, underserved students are told that something is wrong with them, that they are the problem, or something is lacking about them. In the institution of school, students are invalidated when they are told, either explicitly or implicitly, that their home cultural and linguistic behaviors are rude, insubordinate, defiant, disrespectful, disruptive, unmotivated, and lazy (Hollie, 2018). These labels over time chip away at students' cultural and linguistic value in the context of school. To *validate*, therefore, means to provide a counter narrative to students, letting them know in explicit terms that their behaviors are not those negative labels, and that they are being culturally and linguistically misunderstood. According to Hollie (2018):

Affirmation is the intentional and purposeful effort to reverse the negative stereotypes, images, and representations of marginalized cultures and languages promoted by corporate mainstream media, including music, film, and television. The messages are often subtle and play out through the instructional materials, textbooks, and how the Internet is used in schools. To affirm requires intentionally providing images, texts, and narratives that give students alternate perspectives, and the tools to critically analyze media and materials as consumers.

Building is understanding and recognizing the cultural and linguistic behaviors of students and using those behaviors to foster rapport and relationships with the students. In other words, you are building stock with your students, making an investment. Bridging is providing the academic and social skills that students will need to have success beyond your classroom. If building is the investment, then bridging is the return. Bridging is evident when your students demonstrate that they are able to successfully navigate school and mainstream culture. (p. 28)

In sum, validating and affirming cultural and linguistic behaviors provide the counter narrative to the deficit thinking previously described that is historical and institutional (what some would call *systemically racist*), which has led to disproportionality and disparities for marginalized populations, particularly for people of color To *build and bridge* segues that counter narrative by fostering students' cultural assets (not seen as deficits or liabilities) and then making connections between those assets and the academic and social skills necessary for success at school and in mainstream society.

The Purpose

In every classroom, teachers can anticipate, without hesitation, that some students will need to be taught differently, depending on the instructional context. This is the reason why CLR, or VABBing, is necessary. CLR pushes for this necessary pedagogical differentiation for students. Simply put, teachers need cultural responsiveness so they can use diverse methodology to increase their probability of reaching all students, no matter their race, gender, age, economic level, religion, orientation, or ethnic identity (Delpit, 2006; Hammond, 2015). We have dubbed these multiple identities the Rings of Culture, as they become the emanation for which students are culturally validated and affirmed. According to Hollie (2018), "A central focus of CLR is the ethnocultural identity of students, but not to the exclusion of the other 'cultural' identities. In addition to ethnicity, educators have to be responsive to gender culture, orientation culture, national culture, socioeconomic culture, and age culture or the Rings of Culture" (p. 38).

Note that for CLR, the terms *culture* and *language* are defined in the broadest terms and viewed through an anthropological and linguistic lens only, with the understanding that race is not culture (Hollie, 2018; see this source for full definitions and descriptions of these terms). In order to accept CLR as a concept, you must understand the difference between *race* and *culture*. (See Hollie [2018] for a full exposition on these differences.)

According to Hollie (2019a):

> Recognizing the multitude of behaviors as cultural and/or linguistic, and then being responsive to those behaviors during instruction, is the end goal of CLR for educators. In effect, CLR activities [as a pedagogy] tap into who students are based on their cultures of youth culture (Emdin, 2017), their gender culture, their religion culture, and so on. (p. 46)

When teachers incorporate CLR into their instruction, students are empowered to access and explore the curricular content differently. For CLR, the instructional goal is to teach what Harvard professor Andy Molinsky (2013) calls *global dexterity*, which means learning to adapt one's behavior across cultures, or fitting in without giving in. Ultimately, all students must learn what Hollie (2018) calls *situational appropriateness*, which is not a sugar-coated way of saying "fix it," "correct it," or "make it better." Instead, it entails determining what is the most appropriate cultural and linguistic behavior for the situation and doing so without losing one's cultural and linguistic self in the process. Hollie (2019a) states, "Situational appropriateness, as a concept, sounds like the axiomatic *codeswitching*, but it is not the same" (p. 45).

Hollie (2018) explains:

> Situational appropriateness is the concept of determining which cultural or linguistic behaviors are most appropriate for a situation. In other words, students are allowed to make choices around cultural and linguistic behaviors dependent on the situation but without giving up or sacrificing what they consider to be their base culture or language.
>
> Situational appropriateness is the crux of CLR. Understanding the concept will enable you to comprehend the pedagogical underpinnings or, more to the point, enrich the instructional experience for your students as well as yourself. In sum, situational appropriateness is understanding and using the most appropriate cultural or linguistic behaviors for a situation without losing who you are culturally or linguistically.
>
> Related to situational appropriateness is the act of . . . what I call culture-switching. . . . Codeswitching has a very different meaning from that which applies in CLR. In linguistics, the term is usually associated with an action whereby one language is being utilized along with an infusion of the vocabulary of another language into the first language being spoken or written (Gardner-Chloros 2009). Codeswitching in CLR is used more literally and does not carry the pejorative association that is sometimes attached to the term. In the context of CLR, codeswitching is an intentional choice to shift from one linguistic or cultural mode into another one skillfully and

proficiently without giving up, disavowing, or abandoning the home culture or language. . . . I have found that it is harder to make those substitutions or misconstrued meaning with the terms situational appropriateness or culture-switching, so I advocate for those in lieu of codeswitching. (p. 53)

The key takeaway for the purpose of VABB is that *situational appropriateness always requires the validation and affirmation of the student's culture and language first and fore-most*, a recurring theme throughout this book. "The build-and-bridge component of the VABB construct works only when students are validated and affirmed first and [learn] the importance of contextualization, meaning different cultural and linguistic behaviors are required depending on the context" (Hollie, 2019a, p. 45).

The How

Before delving into the *how* of CLR, it's important to remember that entire books have been written on the skills of validating, affirming, building, and bridging (Hollie, 2018; Muhammad & Hollie, 2012). So, in this section, we encapsulate the *how* of CLR pedagogy in figure 1.1, and then explain further through the formula *quantity plus quality plus strategy* or *QQS* (Hollie, 2019a).

CLR Instructional Areas	
CLR Focus on Classroom Management	**CLR Focus on Academic Vocabulary**
CLR Focus on Academic Literacy	**CLR Focus on Academic Language**
CLR Activity Categories	
Classroom Management • Attention signals • Protocols for responding • Protocols for discussing • Movement	**Academic Vocabulary** • Leveled vocabulary words • Personal thesaurus or personal dictionary tools • Vocabulary acquisition strategies • Reinforcement activities and assessments
Academic Literacy • Use of CLR text • Use of engaging read-alouds • Use of effective literacy activities	**Academic Language** • Sentence lifting • Role playing • Retellings • Revising
CLR Activities (For more information about specific CLR activities, see Hollie, 2015.)	
CLR Intent and Purpose (Quantity + Quality + Strategy; Hollie, 2019a)	

FIGURE 1.1: CLR pedagogy encapsulated.

Hollie (2018) identifies four broad instructional areas that educators can infuse with CLR activities under specific CLR activity categories. The overarching goal is for CLR instruction to be infused into daily instruction. CLR itself is not a curriculum but a way of thinking about the how-to of teaching.

Hollie (2018) explains:

> These pedagogical [or instructional] areas represent the general categories that I believe that all classrooms—regardless of grade level or content area—should have in place effectively and efficiently. In my discussion of CLR pedagogy, I include the term *culturally responsive* in the label for each category to ensure that instruction centers on culturally and linguistically appropriate activities. These categories are the basis for instructional failure or success within CLR. CLR does not replace or shield ineffective instruction. Within each pedagogical area are subcategories that depict specific foci for the instruction in that area. These subcategories specify aspects for the teacher to consider when strategically determining how to do various activities. But more importantly, these areas are gatekeepers to success for students, meaning that if your students are not at least proficient or in some cases have mastery in these areas, they will not have success in school. They must be able to manage themselves in the school and classroom contexts, they must increase their academic vocabulary as they matriculate, they must improve their literacy skills, and they must be able to write and speak in academic language. If they do not do these things, they will not make it, regardless of their race or socioeconomic status. This is why I use the four areas because they affect every teacher, regardless of your grade level or content area. (p. 47)

For the purpose of this book, we are only focusing on the CLR category of *culturally responsive classroom management*. For a classroom management approach to be considered culturally responsive, four activity categories must be addressed: ways for responding, ways for discussing, attention signals, and movement activities. In effect, these categories represent proverbial good teaching. Every classroom should have effective and efficient ways of having students discuss topics and respond to questions and prompts. Every classroom should have effective and efficient attention signals to indicate when the teacher needs to bring everyone back after conducting a group discussion. Furthermore, classroom activities should be designed so students can move around the room and interact with classmates for a variety of purposes. In other words, the CLR approach does not require teachers to do anything instructionally unsound. It is only meant to enhance what is already occurring.

A list of activities accompanies each CLR category, giving teachers ample opportunities to choose from based on their student population or instructional context. For example, under attention signals or call and response, there is a recommendation of over fifty call-and-responses activities (Hollie, 2018). The list of possible call-and-response activities is endless and always changing.

Figure 1.2 shows an example of how you can plan CLR instruction based on the CLR pedagogy outlined in figure 1.1 (page 16).

CLR Instructional Area: Classroom Management
CLR Activity Category: Attention Signals
CLR Activity: Call and Response (For example, "When I say 'peace,' you say 'quiet.' Peace, quiet; peace, quiet.")

FIGURE 1.2: Planning specific use of a CLR activity.

What is missing is the fourth layer: CLR Intent and Purpose or Quantity + Quality + Strategy = CLR Success, the CLR formula for success (Hollie, 2019a). *Quantity* means using many different CLR activities with frequency. *Quality* means using the activities with fidelity and technical precision. *Strategy* means knowing when to use a particular activity and for what purpose—to validate and affirm particular cultural and linguistic behaviors and build and bridge to traditional school cultural behaviors (Hollie, 2019a).

Quantity

Quantity, the first step in the formula, requires teachers to develop a CLR activity toolbox. There are many CLR activities teachers can include in their toolboxes (Hollie, 2018). Teachers commonly use these activities in the CLR classroom, and many teachers are already aware of them from sources like Spencer Kagan (Kagan & Kagan, 2009). Many Kagan techniques are well-known and vetted—such as Turn and Talk; Give One, Get One; Campfire Discussion; and Team, Pair, Solo—so teachers tend to be familiar with them (see Kagan & Kagan, 2009, for detailed descriptions). With regular use, these activities eventually become staples in a teacher's CLR toolbox (Hollie, 2019a).

Quality

Quality is the next step in the CLR formula. According to Hollie (2019a), "*Quality* is the use of the CLR activities with fidelity and accuracy. The accurate use of these activities is key to successful implementation of CLR. Adopting the CLR activities and using them regularly can be new learning for some teachers, regardless of their experience" (p. 47). It's critical that teachers know how to conduct the activities accurately and in ways that authentically validate and affirm or build and bridge cultural and linguistic behaviors.

Referring back to the earlier example of call-and-response activities, sometimes teachers mistakenly use them for managing conduct or behavior rather than validating and affirming cultural and linguistic behaviors. For example, the teacher will say a call-and-response prompt, but then respond to students as if he or she simply wants them to be quiet. This use of call and response is more traditional. It should actually signal a gradual quieting for students, in three to five seconds, in order to be sensitive to the social and cultural dynamics of closing a conversation. This nuanced shift is a significant difference in the qualitative use of call and response in a way that is validating and affirming rather than controlling certain conduct. Teachers must use CLR activities with fidelity and accuracy in order to ensure high quality (Hollie, 2019a).

Strategy

Strategy is the last step in the CLR formula of success. What is the *strategy* in using a CLR activity? To say it another way, what is the intentional and purposeful use of the activity? Teachers have three decisions to make, instructionally, when teaching in a culturally and linguistically responsive way (Hollie, 2019a).

1. Is the use of the activity validating and affirming to cultural and linguistic behaviors of the students? If so, which cultural and linguistic behaviors in particular are being validated and affirmed?

2. Is the use of the activity building and bridging the students' cultural behaviors to school cultural behaviors, and if so, which ones? (We will discuss specific cultural and linguistic behaviors later in this chapter.)

3. Is there a balance of activities throughout the lesson that both validate and affirm and build and bridge? (p. 47)

By creating as much balance as possible, teachers automatically reinforce situational appropriateness, because students must decide the most appropriate cultural and linguistic behavior for each situation. Some educators incorrectly think CLR is just a "bucket" of activities. That is not the case. Strategy makes CLR about more than simply using activities. Without strategy, there is no CLR (Hollie, 2019a).

The strategy of CLR is to align specific cultural and linguistic behaviors to specific CLR activities. The basic hypothesis is that the strategic use of a certain activity will equate with the validation and affirmation of a certain behavior or the building and bridging to a school culture behavior. To reiterate, instructional activities can come from a variety of sources (Kagan & Kagan, 2009). Most of the Kagan and Kagan activities are not particularly innovative, but if used effectively and strategically within the context of culture and language, they can make a substantial difference with validation and affirmation. Since cultural and linguistic behaviors are key to being strategic, we will examine the specific cultural and linguistic behaviors on which CLR focuses.

This first section set the course for applying the core principles of CLR and is the foundation to aligning CLR to PBIS. The essence of the core principles is the validation and affirmation of cultural and linguistic behaviors that are the most commonly misunderstood as bad, wrong, or negative behaviors in the context of school culture. In other words, the act of validation and affirmation is the prerequisite to PBIS, or the undergird for supporting underserved students.

Implement an Effective Classroom Management System

Now that we have provided a basic explanation of CLR as an instructional approach, it is time to look at the importance of having an effective schoolwide classroom management system in place. This section is divided into three parts: (1) the importance of an effective classroom management system; (2) a research-based overview of classroom management systems; and (3) classroom management systems aligned with CLR.

The Importance of a Schoolwide Classroom Management System

Some school leaders attempt to solve classroom management problems they do not necessarily want to deal with by sending teachers who are struggling with classroom management to a CLR workshop. However, what these school leaders and teachers quickly find out is that before they can discuss cultural responsiveness and classroom management, they need to establish an effective classroom management system. An ineffective classroom management system cannot be made culturally responsive. Therefore, before creating or even discussing a culturally responsive classroom management system, leaders must take the initial step of deeply reflecting to ascertain the effectiveness of the current classroom management system. In our experience at CLAS, we realized the necessity of a deep reflection the hard way. By all accounts, we were the flagship "culturally responsive" school. People could see CLR in action at CLAS. We had taken a highly theoretical concept and demonstrated its practicality schoolwide. During an interview with visitors to the school, a fifth-grade student said:

> Being at CLAS makes you feel safe. At my other school, kids were always fighting, and teachers didn't care what you did. Here, they make you do your work and care if you don't finish. They teach you about your heritage and about your culture. I really feel that this is where I belong, where I was meant to be. (Orange & Hollie, 2014, p. 64)

In effect, we had the culturally responsive part down, but we learned after the first year that we did not have the classroom management part at all. A myth of cultural responsiveness is that it will cure all ills. At our school, in all our cultural responsiveness, we still had major and minor behavioral challenges, and there were many points along the way when we realized that just being culturally and linguistically responsive was simply not enough.

In several situations, we knew that we needed to put an effective schoolwide classroom management system in place because it would create a distinction between what challenges were better addressed via classroom management versus what could be better addressed through the cultural responsiveness approach. In other words, with a clear classroom management system, we could identify areas that were strictly related to classroom management.

One example of the need for a schoolwide classroom management system was the unevenness in how teachers were consequencing students. Some teachers used very traditional consequences, such as benching students at recess, while others tried to be more progressive or culturally and linguistically responsive about it. The former was an issue because benching students for recess was counter to the CLR philosophy. Keep in mind that the essence of cultural and linguistic responsiveness is the validation and affirmation of cultural and linguistic behaviors. Play, kinesthetic movement, cooperation, and collaboration are behaviors that are inherent with recess. A play break is a natural validation and affirmation, so there was no way we were going to allow benching students for recess at CLAS. But at the same time, we realized that we had to have a system of consequences in place.

A second example of our need for a schoolwide classroom management system was the inconsistency with classroom procedures. As great as they were, our teachers had very different skill levels with the numerous ways of doing and ways of being in the classroom, and they had very different opinions about the value and benefit of being firm, fair, and consistent. By the end of CLAS's first year, we were frustrated, so we spent that summer committed to finding a classroom management system that we could implement the second year. What we learned was that before we could apply the principles of CLR, we had to implement a schoolwide classroom management system.

In your journey to a culturally responsive classroom management approach, you will have to ensure that there is an effective system in place. We researched several options before choosing a system, but unfortunately, it was not as simple as finding "the one" classroom management approach. We needed a system or approach that aligned with CLR. Your system will have to align as well.

Research-Based Overview of Effective Classroom Management Systems

PBIS was not around in 2003, so we had to discover an effective classroom management system based on *research*. As you can imagine, we discovered that there were a lot of different classroom management approaches out there, because an effective classroom management system is at the top of most districts' must-have lists. At that time, our go-to source was Robert Marzano's (2003) *Classroom Management That Works: Research-Based Strategies for Every Teacher*. We have always found Marzano's books, such as *Classroom*

Instruction That Works: Research-Based Strategies for Increasing Student Achievement (Marzano, Pickering, & Pollock, 2001), helpful because they are like one-stop shops. Their meta-analysis approach to research saved us a lot of time, and the information was always practical. We could put it to immediate use.

Prior to consulting Marzano's (2003) work, we had used multiple sources for classroom management from university courses (taught by Sharroky) and from our collective middle school and elementary school teaching experiences. As we will explain later in the chapter, we pulled from a variety of theorists because we could never decide on just one approach. We saw advantages and disadvantages in them all, depending on the day or depending on the student. Therefore, our conceptualization of classroom management was a hodgepodge of viable options from which to choose. We tended to lean toward a somewhat eclectic approach, simply because of the proverbial one-size-never-fits-all concept. At least, that was our rationale at the time. The lesson we learned was that we did not need to be hard-core purists about one approach being more effective than another and neither should you in your search or evaluation of what classroom management system works for you. We considered a stew of different approaches.

Survey of Classroom Management Theorists

In our classroom management stewpot was B. F. Skinner's (1971) behaviorist approach, which Skinner actually never directly related to classroom management or discipline systems. Next in the pot was Jacob Kounin's (1977) approach to improving discipline through lesson management. Kounin is credited for the term *withitness*, which refers to a teacher's omni-awareness of everything that is going on in the classroom. Withitness is a must-have for any effective classroom management system. To round out the theorists, we included Rudolf Dreikurs's theory of discipline through democratic teaching, focused on student self-control and the idea of the democratic classroom (Dreikurs & Cassel, 1990).

While those three theorists provided a philosophical foundation, others offered a practical lens that still resonates to this day. At the top of the list was Lee and Marlene Canter's (1976) *Assertive Discipline*. The Canters' distinctions among assertive, aggressive, and passive discipline, as well as their differences between being proactive and reactive in dealing with behaviors, were significant markers for changing the way we conducted our own classes at CLAS.

When it came to focusing our classroom management system on simply being positive, the go-to was Fred Jones's (1979) positive classroom discipline model. In a nutshell, Jones (1979) states that teachers can encourage "proper" student behavior by helping students gain confidence in their self-control and maintaining a positive attitude. The practical aspects of positive classroom discipline revolve around what Jones (1979) calls *skill clusters*, which are composed of skills that teachers use to prevent or effectively deal with student misbehavior so students productively learn; most notably, these skill clusters include classroom structure, incentive systems, and work with individual students as needed.

To round out our classroom management stew, we used William Glasser's (1998b) noncoercive discipline, Spencer Kagan's (2002) win-win discipline, and Alfie Kohn's (2006) beyond discipline. While Jones focuses on external motivation, Glasser emphasizes internal motivation and students' responsibility for their own behaviors. He is best known for *choice theory*, which helps teachers and students understand human nature and how it influences behavior (Glasser, 1998a). The premise of the theory is that students will work hard and comply with classroom expectations when they get a natural satisfaction from doing so. When teachers only force or externally motivate compliance, then the potential for that satisfaction is lost.

Spencer Kagan, Patricia Kyle, and Sally Scott (2004) are famous for identifying four types of disruptive behaviors that teachers can turn into important learning opportunities, or what we call *teachable moments*; therefore, disciplining students can always be a win-win. True to form, Kagan, Kyle, and Scott (2004) describe the behaviors in a mnemonic—the ABCD of disruptive behavior. *A* stands for aggression, *B* for breaking rules, *C* for confrontation, and *D* for disengagement. The point is that each of the behavior types emanates from a natural and understandable student need, but at the same time, the teacher cannot accept the disruptive behaviors.

Last, but certainly not least, is Alfie Kohn's groundbreaking *Beyond Discipline* (1996, 2006). Kohn stands out because of his critical analysis of schools and how they blame students as the problem. This is a result of Kohn's reliance on constructivist theory as his foundational base. Kohn, therefore, brought our eclectic approach to classroom management full circle, given that we started with B. F. Skinner, since behaviorism is the opposite of constructivism essentially. Kohn's work focuses on schools and classrooms as being communities, which means teachers should build relationships with students, enhance connections with students, jointly undertake classwide and schoolwide activities, and use academic instruction as the classroom management plan and discipline system.

Robert Marzano, the One-Stop Shop

Our potpourri of classroom management approaches was really a literature review, heretofore, and a sign of the times. In the early 2000s, we found that many teachers just winged it when it came to their classroom management. Very few approaches were adopted schoolwide at the time. Many schools left teachers to their own intuition or sent them to a professional learning opportunity about one of the previously described theories. Districts told teachers, "Pick the approach that works for you," which in hindsight was not the best way to go. And that brings us back to Marzano's (2003) work.

To make an investment portfolio analogy, Marzano's (2003) advice is to be less diverse in the various funds and be more focused on a few funds that are low risk but high return. In other words, put your money in the research. Marzano's research identifies seven broad areas that any classroom management system should include, *regardless of the theory*. Table 1.1 shows an overview of these seven key areas for effective classroom management and discipline. Note that some of the previously mentioned theorists, such as Canter and Canter (1976), Glasser (1998a; 1998b), Kohn (1996; 2006), and Kounin (1971), are embedded in Marzano's findings. On the left side of the column are the key principles. On the right side of the column are quotations from Marzano's text that encapsulate the meaning of the principles.

TABLE 1.1: Marzano's Seven Key Areas for Effective Classroom Management and Discipline

Key Areas for Effective Classroom Management and Discipline	Quotes From Marzano's Text
1. Rules and Procedures	"Although the terms are sometimes used interchangeably, rules and procedures have some important differences. Both refer to stated expectations regarding behavior. However, a rule identifies general expectations . . . and a procedure communicates expectations for specific behaviors" (p. 13).
2. Disciplinary Interventions	"It is probably an understatement to say that discipline is on the minds of many teachers. . . . Teachers generally believe that they are not only unprepared to deal with disruptive behavior, but the amount of disruptive behavior in their classes substantially interferes with their teaching" (p. 27).
3. Teacher-Student Relationships	"If a teacher has a good relationship with students, then students more readily accept the rules and procedures and disciplinary actions that follow their violations" (p. 41).
4. Mental Set	"Effective managers approach the classroom with a specific frame of mind—a specific mental set. The construct of a mental set in classroom management is quite similar to the construct of 'mindfulness' in psychology" (p. 65).
5. Students' Responsibility for Management	"Students should be given the message that they are responsible for their own behavior and that they should be provided with strategies and training to realize that control" (p. 77).
6. Getting Off to a Good Start	"Research points to the beginning of the school year as the linchpin for effective classroom management" (p. 92).
7. Management at the School Level	"School-level management and classroom-level management have a symbiotic relationship that is probably best understood if we consider the perspective of an individual student" (p. 103).

Source: Marzano, 2003.

Now armed with the general principles that encapsulate effective classroom management, based on research as well as learning from our previous experiences and research, we at CLAS were ready to decide what classroom management approach would be the best fit for our students. This will be your next step as well.

Following is a quick recap of how we arrived at this fork in the road. Our cornerstone was to be authentically culturally and linguistically responsive, but we also realized that we needed more than CLR to have overall success. We needed a schoolwide classroom management system, but whatever system we chose, it had to be aligned or malleable with our philosophy. Thus, there are two take-away questions for your consideration. Is the classroom management system effective and research based, and is it congruent with your general philosophy?

Classroom Management Systems Aligned With CLR

After an exhaustive search, we landed on two classroom management approaches and a character development program. The first came from Jim Fay and David Funk's (1995) *Teaching With Love and Logic: Taking Control of the Classroom*. Fay and Funk's platform is based on four key principles: (1) enhance self-control, (2) share the control, (3) balance consequence with empathy, and (4) share the thinking. The second, which is more a system than an approach, came from Randy Sprick's (2009) *CHAMPS: A Proactive and Positive Approach to Classroom Management, Second Edition*. Some would argue that CHAMPS is the precursor to PBIS. The abbreviation for CHAMPS means the following.

- *C* stands for "conversation" and refers to whether students can talk during the procedure or activity and, if so, how loudly and with whom.
- *H* stands for "help" and refers to how students are to solicit help from the teacher or classmates.
- *A* stands for "activity" and refers to the directions for what students are to do.
- *M* stands for "movement" and refers to whether students can move during the procedure or activity and, if so, how and when.
- *P* stands for "participation" and refers to what active student participation looks like.
- *S* stands for "success" and refers to a successful experience from following the CHAMPS expectations delineated for the specific procedure or instructional activity (Sprick, 2009).

We used love and logic as our approach to discipline and CHAMPS as our schoolwide classroom management system because we liked that the former was principles based and the latter was systems based. CLR in its foundation is based on principles but at the same time functions most effectively in a structure.

A third important component of our culturally responsive classroom management approach was a focus on character development—the righteous principles. In most instances, schools that have comprehensive classroom management systems will have a values-based component that promotes and reinforces attributes like kindness, respect, and patience. We based our righteous principles on the seven principles of Ma'at, based in Kemetic history and the Egyptian goddess by the same name (Browder, 1992). The seven principles are (1) balance, (2) truth, (3) order, (4) justice, (5) harmony, (6) reciprocity, and (7) propriety. We leveraged these principles for building character, community, and a school culture at CLAS, meaning we centered our classroom management and discipline system on the righteous principles. We ended up calling our culturally responsive classroom management system Ways of Being, Ways of Doing. Daniel created cartoon characters to go along with the righteous principles, called the Scribes. Each character was one of the principles, in look and design, as we tried to connect to our students via youth culture. Figure 1.3 shows the Scribes of the Righteous Principles.

The Scribes of the Righteous Principles

| Rashida | Raekwan | C. J. | Matthew | Malik | Rhonette | Paulo |
| **Balance** | **Truth** | **Order** | **Justice** | **Harmony** | **Reciprocity** | **Propriety** |

Source: © 2003 by Daniel Russel Jr. Used with permission.

FIGURE 1.3: The Scribes of the Righteous Principles.

Figure 1.4 outlines the key components of love and logic, CHAMPS, and the righteous principles, and how they fit within the CLAS philosophy. The premises in the first row speak to a philosophical gateway between each approach and CLR. The second row features each approach's own set of principles; some, not all, fit with CLR in one way or another. For example, CHAMPS emphasizes external rewards, whereas CLR does not. The platforms in the third row simply mean the framework or structure of each approach.

Criteria	Love and Logic	CHAMPS	Righteous Principles
Premises	Reduce the need for discipline based on a principles approach versus a systems approach.	Structure and organize the classroom to have a huge impact on student behavior.	Maintain peace and goodness in the universe (school).
Principles	Maintain consistency in the principles approach, adhering to a set of values rather than treating everyone the same.	Apply firm and fair classroom routines; positive, caring interactions; extrinsic motivation to promote excellence; and clear standards of behavior.	Ensure students look to these principles for guidance in keeping peace and goodness in the classroom and school.
Platforms	Implement the four key principles: (1) enhance self-control, (2) share the control, (3) balance consequence with empathy, and (4) share the thinking.	Implement the eight modules: (1) vision, (2) organization, (3) expectations, (4) the first month, (5) motivation, (6) monitor and revise, (7) correction procedures, and (8) classwide motivation systems.	Correlate the seven principles to love and logic and CHAMPS for consistency, balance, order, harmony, propriety, reciprocity, justice, and truth.
Practices	Understand the differences between consequences and punishment. Determine consequences with empathy and delayed or wait time through a process of shared control and thinking.	Establish learning-activity accountability and what students will do. • Conversation • Help • Activity • Movement • Participation	Align the seven principles to classroom practices and realities (for example, harmony means helping and sharing with one another).
Particulars	Focus not so much on what you want students to do but on what you do as adults (core beliefs).	Ensure that different classes and students receive different levels of structure and systems (low, medium, and high).	Ensure public recognition (the righteous ceremony) comes through student reflection and adult observation. Recognize every student for something.

Source: Adapted from Fay & Funk, 1995; adapted from Sprick, 2009.

FIGURE 1.4: Congruent components for CLR.

*Visit **go.SolutionTree.com/diversityandequity** for a free reproducible version of this figure.*

The selection of practices speaks to the ins and outs of the approach and what we could use in terms of daily implementation and overall application. Finally, the last row features the particulars—what some would call the specifics—for each approach. Combined, these were the congruent components for CLR at CLAS.

For each selected approach, we required the following four fundamental premises that we dubbed the *four As*: (1) allowance, (2) ability, (3) aim, and (4) appreciation. These premises provided a rationale for the process we ultimately used to make the selections.

1. The *allowance* to validate and affirm each student, as an individual, culturally and linguistically, meaning each approach allowed for such opportunities.
2. The *ability* to empower each student's social and emotional development by developing character traits, as outlined by the righteous principles.
3. The *aim* of building strong, positive relationships evidenced by an intentional series of positive interactions throughout students' matriculation
4. The *appreciation* of teaching academic and social skills necessary for cross-cultural environments, without devaluing or minimizing each student's own culture.

Now, the question is, what will your congruent classroom management system be? Our intent here is not to endorse any of these particular approaches or, for that matter, take a deep dive into each one. The objective is to illustrate what worked for our situation as the flagship laboratory school for cultural responsiveness and emphasize that in order for you to have a culturally responsive classroom management system, you need to discover what works for you, your students, your staff, and your care providers. For us, choosing a classroom management system was about finding the right fit, like trying on a pair of shoes. We knew our shoe size—being culturally responsive—but we had to buy shoes that fit. This is not an exact science by any measure. Looking at the core principles of CLR and effective classroom management, we can only describe what fits our own situation. You will have to choose based on your own situation as well. Too many times in education, people try to replicate what someone else has done, when they should be trying to create what works for them.

Once you have an effective classroom management system in place, there is another very important process to consider, because having an effective culturally responsive classroom management system is necessary but not sufficient. You still need a process for determining which behaviors are cultural and which behaviors are unacceptable, with the goal of finding out which specific cultural behaviors seem to trigger teachers and lead to what we call *cultural misunderstandings*. These misunderstandings can ultimately lead to unwarranted punishment and consequences, like time-outs, send-outs (referrals), or worse. The last section of this chapter describes a process for determining whether behaviors are cultural or unacceptable.

Determine What Behaviors Are Cultural and What Behaviors Are Not Acceptable

After accepting what CLR is as its own brand compared to other types of cultural responsiveness, and then implementing an effective classroom management system that fits your school's goals for classroom management and discipline, the final step is deciding which behaviors are cultural and which are not acceptable. Cultural behaviors should be validated and affirmed, *not* punished or made negative. In our work with schools across the United States, we consider this step as an essential link in the chain to alignment with PBIS. There can be no alignment to PBIS without separating cultural behaviors from other types of behaviors and then committing to the validation and affirmation in how you talk with, relate to, and ultimately teach students.

Following are the three steps for determining cultural behaviors as compared to unacceptable behaviors, and then practicing validation and affirmation with those behaviors.

1. Know and understand the cultural behaviors for what they are, from an anthropological perspective, as explained in the first section of the chapter. (For a full description and deep examination of cultural behaviors, see Muhammad and Hollie [2012] or Hollie [2018], or visit the Cultural Behavior and Tutorial Bundle website at https://vabbacademy.thinkific.com /bundles/cultural-behavior-tutorial-bundle.)

2. Reach consensus as a staff about which cultural behaviors you will validate and affirm and which behaviors you will consider as not cultural and, therefore, are unacceptable or egregious.

3. Begin practicing specific ways you will validate and affirm the cultural behaviors (Hollie, 2018).

Commonly Misunderstood Cultural and Linguistic Behaviors

Hollie (2019a) writes, "Focusing on cultural and linguistic behaviors builds on the proactive approach of utilizing validating and affirming engagement activities to culturally and linguistically appeal to students" (p. 48). Students are validated and affirmed based on certain culturally and linguistically defined behaviors in relation to the types of activities teachers use. According to Hollie (2019a), the following cultural and linguistic behaviors build off two solid research bases grounded in anthropology: (1) the iceberg concept of culture (Sussman, 2014), which establishes the focus on culture as opposed to only looking through a racial lens; and (2) which cultural and linguistic behaviors are most likely *not* to be validated and affirmed in the milieu of school culture and classroom dynamics (Boykin, 1983). The iceberg concept refers to a superficial perspective of culture (the top of the iceberg) as opposed to a deep perspective of culture (the below-the-line, or underwater part of the iceberg). The focus of CLR is on deep cultural behaviors (below the line) (Hollie, 2019a; Sussman, 2014).

The following is not an exhaustive list, and we recommend referring to Hollie's previous text (2018) for a fuller explanation of the cultural and linguistic behaviors. Other cultural behaviors can and do occur. The takeaway is that all of us exhibit cultural behaviors depending on our heritage (ethnic identity), upbringing, and where we were raised. These behaviors are not race dependent. The CLR educator needs to be familiar with these behaviors to validate and affirm students. Hollie (2019a) states:

> It is important to conceptualize these behaviors without thinking about them in the context or comparison of school or mainstream culture only. They are meant to stand alone, have value on their own, and be representative of who the students are culturally and linguistically for validating and affirming purposes. To only see these behaviors in relation to school culture misses the point and treads on deficit thinking. (p. 49)

1. **Eye contact:** We communicate with our eyes. Depending on our cultural identity, we can show disrespect or respect, attention or lack of attention, or intrigue or non-intrigue by how long we maintain eye contact (known as maintenance).

2. **Proximity:** The distance between two people is often culturally dependent because it is a way of showing respect, rapport, and relationship. The appropriate distance is culturally determined, whether a person is asking a question, seeking information, or simply wanting to relate through conversation; all affect proximity. The distance and purpose vary from culture to culture.

3. **Kinesthetic (high movement):** *Kinesthetic* refers to moving while learning, being tactile with use of gross motor skills, moving the big muscles, and learning through physical activities. Some cultures learn better while moving.

4. **Cooperative or collaborative (shared work and responsibility):** Working together and sharing responsibility to contribute to the overall performance is very important is some cultures as compared to working individually in other cultures.

5. **Spontaneous (impromptu, impulsive):** People can demonstrate culture preferences by being impulsive and improvisational, the tendency to respond as coming or resulting from an immediate or natural impulse; unplanned as compared to being prompted or planned out.

6. **Pragmatic language use (nonverbal):** Eye contact, hand gestures, facial expressions, and body language can sometimes communicate more than verbal language. In some cultures, the emphasized use of non-verbals can be more meaningful, depending on the context and what needs to be communicated.

7. **Realness (direct versus indirect):** Realness refers to how truthful, authentic, and direct we are in our communications. Different cultures value different levels of directness. How truth and authenticity are communicated to others can be culturally based.

8. **Conversational patterns (verbal overlap and non-linearity):** Verbal overlapping while someone else is talking shows engagement and focus for some languages and cultures, while in other cultures, not overlapping can show the same levels of engagement.

9. **Orality and verbal expressiveness (verve):** *Verve* refers to *how* someone says something, not *what* he or she says. Verve happens when the combination of emphasized use of non-verbals and verbal expressiveness occur simultaneously.

10. **Sociocentrism (social interaction to learn):** In some cultures, social interaction is more valued than the content being discussed and is a contributing variable to the learning. This is sometimes referred to as *learning by talking* (socializing).

11. **Communalism (collective success):** In a communal culture, the concept of *we* is more important than *I*. The success of the whole (community, family, class, collaborative group) outweighs and is more valued than the success of the individual.

12. **Subjectivity (relativity):** Subjectivity means the essential understanding of a topic or concept lies in relativity, perspective, and granularity, not just right and wrong. In some cultures, multiple perspectives are allowed and valued.

13. **Concept of time (precise or relative):** We can view time conceptually as precise, meaning the clock controls the beginning and ending of an event or occurrence. Or, we can view time as relative. Human interactions (what is happening in the moment) control the event or occurrence, not the clock. Some cultures value relative time more than conceptual time.

14. **Dynamic attention span (multiple ways to show focus):** This refers to how we demonstrate varied ways of showing focus and task orientation, depending not only on ethnic cultures but also age and gender cultures.

15. **Field dependent (relevance):** This is the orientation toward external defined goals and reinforcements compared to the social and cultural relevance to one's own experiences. If one is field dependent, contextualization matters and is highly valued.

16. **Immediacy (connectedness):** Immediacy refers to actions that all at once communicate warmth, acceptance, closeness, and availability. Connectedness and sense of immediacy can be the tendency to evaluate situations through a lens of urgency. In the classroom, students who value immediacy want to know about things *now*, and having to wait creates stress (Hollie, 2019b).

These commonly misunderstood and misinterpreted cultural behaviors are the basis for understanding a CLR approach. The full discernment of the CLR approach comes with acknowledging the hidden biases we all have around race and culture (Chugh, 2018). The bottom line is that, even when provided with anthropological research to back up the validity of the cultural and linguistic behaviors, just knowing about or understanding the cultural behaviors is necessary but insufficient. Your staff will need to have deep, courageous, and honest conversations about their collective biases against these behaviors as related to school culture, or what we call *school institutionality*. In the following section, we explore what staff must consider when discussing the cultural and linguistic behavior of *sociocentrism*.

Sociocentrism

Sociocentrism is one of the most misunderstood cultural and linguistic behaviors. (It appears tenth in the list of common cultural behaviors on pages 30–31.) It often leads to students being unfairly disciplined in class with admonishments, time-outs, or out-of-class referrals marked *disruptive*. What is *sociocentrism*? Literally, it means that the act of socializing or being social is central to the person at the time. By the way, this is not a dictionary definition. This definition comes from an anthropological and linguistic viewpoint (Boykin, 1983), as well as common sense.

The CLR lens is in direct opposition to any deficit thinking and boldly, but respectfully, refutes a singular dominant culture's viewpoint. With that said, sociocentrism, in the teaching-learning dynamic, values talking or socializing while learning. Numerous cultures around the world accept and appreciate this dynamic (Kaplan & Grabe, 2002). What mainstream culture calls *ramblings* are considered as examples of sociocentrism in CLR. For some, learning by talking, socializing, and engaging in ways that support a focus on the social exchange can be more important than the content itself.

Teachers who do not come from sociocentric cultures can misunderstand or misconstrue students who come from sociocentric cultures as being too talkative, disruptive, off task, and chatty, or, in some cases, as having attention deficit hyperactivity disorder (ADHD). These misunderstandings often lead to negative exchanges between the teacher and the student, which prevent positive, strong relationships on the one hand and drive up disproportionality and disparity on the other hand. Countless students, in stories that have largely gone untold, are being punished, referred out, and even suspended for simply being who they are, which is culturally sociocentric.

Distinguishing cultural behaviors from unacceptable behaviors requires an understanding and eventual acceptance of said behaviors as cultural. Without understanding and acceptance, misunderstandings and hidden biases will remain, which means continuing an unresponsive situation for students in the long term. Clarity on these behaviors is of utmost importance in learning to accept them.

The Importance of Clarity on and Acceptance of Cultural Behaviors

Regarding cultural behaviors, clarity is more important than agreement most of the time, so it is important to always seek clarity first and then decide whether there is agreement or not. Acceptance is the ultimate goal. The degree to which people agree on and accept the validity of the cultural behaviors is based on each person's belief system. In other words, it is almost impossible to get everyone on the same page because each person is going to be at a different place in terms of their beliefs about each behavior and the specific situational context discussed. Your goal, therefore, should be staff consensus. We define *consensus* as a general agreement among most people but not everybody, and it means that even if someone does not agree with it, he or she can still live with the decision. While you do not need everybody to agree, you do need at least 60 percent of staff to move forward and put your school in a position to be successful (Chugh, 2018).

In Sharroky's professional developments on culturally responsive classroom management, he has an activity called Three Columns, which facilitates discussion around cultural behaviors to assist staff in reaching consensus. It is meant to challenge mindsets and blind spots. The directions for the activity are as follows.

1. Project a copy of the Three Columns template for school staff (see figure 1.5, page 34). Staff members will place at least two behaviors in each column. Inform staff the goal is to commit to validating and affirming the behaviors deemed cultural but are not situationally appropriate in column 1, and to consistently and fairly use progressive disciplinary practices with column 2. (Note that *culturally inappropriate* does not mean "bad" or "wrong"; it means situational or contextual. The cultural behavior is not appropriate for the *context*, meaning the time or place.) Column 3 is exclusively used for zero-tolerance behaviors, such as those that deal with safety and legalities.

2. Refer to the cultural behaviors list (pages 30–31) to decide which two cultural behaviors you want to focus on as a staff (with 60–80 percent agreement). We suggest that you focus on two behaviors every four to six weeks. Whatever behaviors you agree on, the group must commit to validate and affirm those cultural behaviors and not go negative, consequential, or punitive.

3. Column 2 behaviors are for your classroom management and discipline system or, in PBIS terms, major disruptions versus minor disruptions. Typically, minor disruptions are dealt with in class, while major disruptions might require intervention outside the classroom.

4. Column 3 tends to be the easiest, most straightforward one to fill out. Here, you are talking about behaviors that are illegal or involve safety issues.

Cultural Behaviors	Unacceptable Behaviors	Egregious Behaviors

FIGURE 1.5: Three Columns activity template.

*Visit **go.SolutionTree.com/diversityandequity** for a free reproducible version of this figure.*

The whole point of the activity, and the reason why schools need culturally responsive classroom management, is to validate and affirm cultural and linguistic behaviors that the school culture, as an institution, does not.

The Practice of Validation and Affirmation

After you complete step 2, reach consensus as a staff about which cultural behaviors to validate and affirm and which you consider not cultural (or unacceptable; see page 29), you must make a commitment to validate and affirm those cultural behaviors. In sum, you can validate and affirm students' cultural and linguistic behaviors by changing how staff talk to students, relate to students, and teach students when these behaviors are at play. The practice of validation and affirmation as a skill set of CLR is described in *The Will to Lead, the Skill to Teach* (Muhammad & Hollie, 2012).

Most times, simply not going negative, punitive, or consequential around cultural and linguistic behaviors is validating and affirming in itself. But the power of validation and affirmation lies in saying words like *honor, appreciate, love, relate, value,* or *connect* when students are demonstrating cultural behaviors. As an example, let's return to the behavior of sociocentrism. If a teacher notices a student being sociocentric while working in a discussion group, the teacher can validate and affirm the student by saying something like, "I love how engaged you are in the discussion," instead of, "Stay on topic." This validating and affirming statement can be a difference maker for a teacher's interactions and relationships with students.

Relationships are a powerful variable in student achievement (Hattie, 2012), and CLR is premised on building strong and meaningful relationships with students that have a long-lasting impact. Acknowledging and valuing students' cultural assets and not always focusing on liabilities build strong relationships, while thinking of cultural assets as liabilities and describing them as wrong, bad, or lacking build weak relationships (Hollie, 2018). When you genuinely validate and affirm students in the teaching-learning dynamic, they feel valued not only in the context of the academic setting, but also in relation to the teacher or adult in the room.

You can leverage strong relationships during challenging times or breakdowns between you and students. The importance of strong relationships was evident during the 2020 COVID-19 pandemic and school closures. Teachers who had strong relationships with their students pre-pandemic could leverage those relationships when they needed to reach students virtually. Sadly, teachers who did not have strong relationships could not, as reported by the students (Los Angeles Unified School District, 2020). Some students claimed that teachers had not tried to connect with them before, so why now? Validating and affirming students equal strong relationships, which makes a difference when you need to leverage the relationship with a student.

The final way to validate and affirm cultural behaviors is to teach differently rather than traditionally. You can find a CLR skill set in *Culturally and Linguistically Responsive Teaching and Learning: Classroom Practices for Student Success* (Hollie, 2018), which provides a list of methodologies and activities that allow teachers to validate and affirm their students by how they teach. The hypothesis behind CLR is that by matching certain activities with the variety of cultural behaviors, teachers automatically validate and affirm students through the learning experience. Looking at the cultural behavior of sociocentrism, teachers could use various discussion protocols, such as Campfire Discussion or Four Corners, as primary ways to honor some students' norm of socializing while learning. Teachers could also honor this norm by maintaining the recommended talk ratio of 35 percent teacher talk to 65 percent student talk, meaning students are doing most of the talking while learning more than two-thirds of the time (Hollie, 2018).

Think of your learning throughout the years and the classes in which you felt validated and affirmed, regardless of the reason. We call that feeling *empowerment and liberation*, which should be the end result of CLR, especially in the context of classroom management.

Conclusion

After reading this chapter, there should be no doubt about the importance of foundational CLR knowledge regarding culturally responsive classroom management. The learning that comes from the following chapters cannot happen without knowing how to apply the core principles of CLR, which were explained in the first section of the chapter. It's also essential to have an effective classroom management system in place. We reviewed the research-based principles and important theorists in classroom management as well as guidance for how to research and select the best classroom management system for your situation. In the final section, we provided a process for differentiating between cultural and linguistic behaviors and unacceptable behaviors, which is the essence of effective culturally responsive classroom management. With the foundation in place, we can now turn to earnestly authentically aligning CLR to PBIS, which is covered in the next chapter.

CHAPTER 2

PBIS and Authentic Cultural and Linguistic Responsiveness

"MY JOURNEY TO CULTURALLY AND LINGUISTICALLY RESPONSIVE PBIS" DANIEL RUSSELL JR.

My journey to culturally and linguistically responsive PBIS began in my early years of teaching at my first school. As with most if not all beginning teachers, I was struggling with effective classroom management and sought answers for how to be more successful. I initially was influenced by Lee Canter's (1992) assertive discipline model and gradually developed better classroom management. However, I began to feel that my discipline approach, which was primarily based on enforcing compliance through rewards and punishment, was increasingly at odds with what I was learning about being a CLR educator. This growing dissatisfaction led to a desire to change my mindset and practices regarding discipline, so I began to explore other approaches.

A colleague introduced me to Marvin Marshall's (2007) book Discipline Without Stress, Punishments, or Rewards: How Teachers and Parents Promote Responsibility and Learning, *which I found to be more aligned with what I understood as CLR. Then, I added what I learned from Fay and Funk's (1995)* Teaching with Love and Logic *and Randy Sprick's (2009) CHAMPS approach, as well as what Lisa Delpit (2012) describes as being a warm demander. These approaches, along with others, became foundational pieces of the culturally responsive schoolwide discipline approach we co-developed and came to call Ways of Doing, Ways of Being at CLAS. However, I was unaware that we were essentially developing a form of culturally responsive PBIS.*

For me, the explicit connection between CLR and PBIS came after a major transition in my career. After twenty-one years as a classroom teacher, I opted to take on the role of dean of students. My first major task was to implement PBIS in the grades K–6 school at which I was working. After receiving training and professional development in PBIS, I asked myself the same questions I had asked of the other approaches to student discipline:

- *"Does this approach work for students from historically underserved backgrounds (for example, Black and Latinx)?"*

- *"Is this approach authentically culturally and linguistically responsive?"*

I found, unsurprisingly, that PBIS could be effective for underserved students, but only if it was implemented in a culturally responsive way. Furthermore, I learned that PBIS was not inherently culturally responsive but could be made so.

For the next several years, as the focus of my doctorate, I studied how and why to implement PBIS in a culturally responsive way. Sharroky and I then discovered that we had been on parallel pathways in terms of the need for aligning PBIS with CLR. This revelation led us to combine our efforts in developing a culturally responsive schoolwide discipline approach, as we had done at CLAS. We built on our precursor to CLR-PBIS, what we called Ways of Doing, Ways of Being, to write this book. I know my journey to culturally and linguistically responsive PBIS is not over, as I have embraced the understanding that there is always more to learn.

In our work with educators that we train and coach in CLR through the Center for Culturally Responsive Teaching and Learning, numerous teachers and staff shared their experiences with us regarding the ineffectiveness of PBIS with their underserved students, despite the implementation of PBIS, often with fidelity. In particular, they shared their continued struggles with the persistent overrepresentation of Black students in office discipline referrals and suspensions at their schools. These most likely were the result of challenges teachers faced with understanding the difference between cultural behaviors and unacceptable ones. For example, in one district with which we worked, Black students were suspended more than four times as often as White students, even though PBIS was in place. Furthermore, they shared with us that this disparity was amplified when considering the intersection of race and special education status. Black students identified with special needs were documented as being removed from the education environment at higher rates than all other demographic groups. Again, this is even with the faithful implementation of PBIS—a clear indicator of a systemic problem.

What teachers shared with us mirrored what the aforementioned literature and research reveal about PBIS's lack of effectiveness with underserved students, as evidenced by racial disparities in exclusionary discipline (Betters-Bubon, Brunner, & Kansteiner, 2016; Bradshaw, Mitchell, & Leaf, 2010; Kaufman et al., 2010; Vincent & Tobin, 2011). This revelation caused us to wonder why PBIS is not as effective for underserved students. What we learned through the literature was that part of the problem is that PBIS is not authentically culturally and linguistically responsive.

We are not saying PBIS does not have value, as ample empirical research has proven it does (Barrett, Bradshaw, & Lewis, 2008; Bohanon et al., 2006; Bradshaw et al., 2010; Bradshaw, Reinke, Brown, Bevans, & Leaf, 2008; Caldarella, Shatzer, Gray, Young, & Young, 2011; Noltemeyer, Petrasek, Stine, Palmer, Meehan, & Jordan, 2018; Tyre & Feuerborn, 2011). Rather, our intent, in this chapter, is to explain why PBIS is not authentically culturally responsive so you can better understand how to make it so. This perspective also contrasts with what Milaney Leverson, Kent Smith, Kent McIntosh, Jennifer Rose, and Sarah Pinkelman (2019) assert in their *PBIS Cultural Responsiveness Field Guide*. Although we agree that cultural responsiveness is a core component of PBIS and PBIS is not fully implemented unless done so in a culturally responsive manner, we disagree with their stance that using a term such as *culturally responsive PBIS* (CR-PBIS) "suggests that CR-PBIS is something distinct from PBIS" (p. 2). For us, because PBIS is not authentically culturally responsive, it is distinct from a culturally and linguistically responsive PBIS. Therefore, unequivocally, school leaders and teachers need clarity on why PBIS is not inherently culturally and linguistically responsive and how they can adapt it to be that way.

In this chapter, we explain the reasons, revealed by literature, why PBIS is not authentically culturally and linguistically responsive. It begins with the emergence of the need for a positive and proactive school discipline framework and a brief history of PBIS's origin, development, and national diffusion within this context. After the historical context is set, we provide five rationales for why PBIS is not authentically culturally and linguistically responsive.

A Shift From Punitive to Positive

As classroom practitioners and school-site leaders, we are constantly seeking how to most effectively manage student behavior in the classroom, on the playground, in the hallways, and in all areas across the school campus. We have sought answers on how best to respond when students invariably make behavioral choices that negatively affect themselves, their classmates, or their school community. We also have looked for solutions for how to make our campuses safer and equitable for all students. Our searches have led to varying and even diametrically opposing approaches that have trended with the social and political conditions of the time.

From the 1980s to the early 2000s, schools and districts, paralleling the criminal justice system, adopted zero-tolerance policies that focused on punitive practices. With this discipline paradigm, the belief was that harsher consequences, even for relatively minor behaviors, would result in better student behavior and safer schools. Yet, the effectiveness of this punitive approach has not been backed by empirical research (Scott, 2018; U.S. Commission on Civil Rights, 2019; Whitford, Katsiyannis, & Counts, 2016).

Numerous researchers have asserted that punitive practices do not work, they do not increase school safety, and they actually worsen outcomes, particularly for underserved students (Allen & Steed, 2016; Mallett, 2016). In fact, according to the *2015–2016 Civil Rights Data Collection* survey (U.S. Department of Education Office for Civil Rights, 2018), under the zero-tolerance approach to discipline adopted by 94 percent of U.S. public schools (Monroe, 2005), Black and Latinx students were disproportionately overrepresented in suspensions and expulsions as compared to White students. Additionally, research has attributed the emergence of the school-to-prison pipeline in the 1980s—which has had a disparate impact on Black and Latinx students, particularly those identified with special needs—to these zero-tolerance policies (Castillo, 2014; Dancy, 2014; Grace & Nelson, 2019). The school-to-prison pipeline is the criminalizing process whereby students who have been the recipients of exclusionary discipline, often more than once, are funneled by educators from schools into the criminal justice system (Dancy, 2014).

In response to this failure and harm of the zero-tolerance approach, beginning in the 1990s to early 2000s, educators in U.S. schools began to shift from these punitive policies and practices to positive and proactive approaches (Ritter, 2018). Moreover, research shows that positive and proactive approaches to discipline are more effective at creating safe and equitable school environments (Bottiani, Bradshaw, & Gregory, 2018; Reinke, Herman, & Stormont, 2013). In fact, the American Federation of Teachers publicly renounced the use of zero-tolerance practices and advocates for more empirically effective alternatives to punitive practices (Skiba & Losen, 2015). Restorative justice (alternatively referred to as *restorative practices*), logical consequences, and trauma-informed practices are a few examples of these positive and proactive approaches.

The widely implemented PBIS framework has been leading this antipodal shift in school discipline paradigms since the late 1990s. According to the Center on PBIS (2021b), as of 2018, PBIS was being implemented in nearly 28,000, or about 25 percent of, schools across the United States. As of 2018, California, our home state, had nearly 2,500 schools using a PBIS framework, and twenty-one U.S. states had at least five hundred schools using PBIS (Georgia Department of Education, 2018).

In order to understand PBIS's ascendance as the most diffusely applied positive and proactive approach to school discipline in the United States (Center on PBIS, 2021b), it is important to take a brief look at its origin and subsequent history. The next section traces how PBIS got its start in federal laws passed to protect the civil rights of students with special needs and in the work of the U.S. Department of Education. This is followed by the influence of federal policies and grant money made available to schools for improving school climate and culture and mitigating disproportionality in exclusionary discipline. Last, we reveal the paradox, or what we call the *open secret*, of PBIS's overall effectiveness in improving school safety and reducing the need for punitive practices, yet its limited success at creating equity in school discipline and welcoming school environments for underserved students.

The History of PBIS Diffusion

So, how did the PBIS framework come to be used in thousands of individual schools and districts across the United States? PBIS, alternatively referred to as *schoolwide positive behavioral interventions and supports* (*SWPBIS*) and *positive behavioral supports* (*PBS*), was developed in the late 1990s by researchers out of the University of Oregon (Goodman-Scott, Hays, & Cholewa, 2018). Educators had known about prevention-based approaches for addressing problematic student behaviors since the 1970s but they had not yet been implemented on a wide scale (Sugai & Horner, 2002).

In 1997, the U.S. federal government passed the Individuals With Disabilities Education Act (IDEA), which included provisions for schools to adopt positive and preventive disciplinary practices in order to address the overrepresentation of students with special needs in exclusionary discipline (Bal, 2015; Goodman-Scott et al., 2018). In response to IDEA, researchers at the University of Oregon developed the PBIS framework and a federally funded national center to support schools, districts, and states with their implementation of PBIS, called the Office of Special Education Programs (OSEP) Technical Assistance Center on Positive Behavioral Interventions and Supports (Goodman-Scott et al., 2018). In 2004, IDEA was reauthorized with added requirements that schools address racial disproportionality in exclusionary discipline (Bal, 2015). Moreover, PBIS was the only schoolwide disciplinary approach specifically mentioned in IDEA 2004 (Bal, 2015), and this near endorsement had profound ramifications for PBIS's subsequent national diffusion.

Although use of PBIS itself is not legally mandated, U.S. schools and districts have been required by the U.S. Department of Education since the late 1990s to move toward a positive and proactive behavioral approach in order to comply with IDEA. Additionally, according to Christina A. Samuels (2013), the widespread increase in use of PBIS has in part been incentivized by former president Barack Obama's Race to the Top educational reform plan. During President Obama's administration, schools and districts could obtain funding to improve school climate through Race to the Top grants, particularly to address inequities in discipline data in compliance with IDEA 2004's provision that schools mitigate racial disparities in exclusionary discipline. Furthermore, according to a fact sheet by Partners for Dignity and Rights (2021), PBIS was specifically highlighted "as a transformation model for turning around a state's lowest achieving schools." Thus, the combination of legal compliance with IDEA, possible access to federal funding, and research showing the ineffectiveness of punitive policies created the conditions for PBIS's expansive growth.

Since the early 2000s, the PBIS approach has demonstrated its effectiveness in reducing exclusionary discipline and shifting teachers, schools, and districts toward a nonpunitive approach (Sugai, O'Keeffe, & Fallon, 2012). Yet, as previously noted, this success has not been all-inclusive (Sugai et al., 2012; Vincent, Sprague, CHiXapkaid, Tobin, & Gau, 2015). In other words, the data show that PBIS has worked for some students but not equitably for all students. Despite PBIS's documented success, data for schools and districts implementing the PBIS framework reveal that Black and Latinx students have continued to be disproportionately represented in exclusionary discipline (Vincent & Tobin, 2011). Why, then, has this approach not consistently shown the same effectiveness with historically underserved and marginalized students as it has with the demographically dominant group (specifically, White students)? We argue that this discrepancy exists because PBIS was not originally culturally and linguistically responsive in its inception and its intention. The next section outlines the reasons for this argument.

The Need for Authenticity

Lefki Kourea, Ya-Yu Lo, and Tosha Owens (2016) assert that PBIS can become culturally and linguistically responsive by considering students' different cultural backgrounds. Therefore, we can conclude that PBIS is not inherently culturally and linguistically responsive because it needs to be adapted in order to have cultural responsiveness. We can even infer that PBIS is not authentically culturally responsive because the original developers of PBIS advise that it should be made so by educators. George Sugai, Breda O'Keeffe, and Lindsay Fallon (2012) state that "implementation can be enhanced further by considering the cultural context and learning history of students and family, faculty, and community members" (p. 204). The Center on PBIS (2021e) also describes this need for adapting PBIS for cultural responsiveness by ensuring that each school's PBIS has cultural and contextual fit.

Cultural and contextual fit includes the following elements:

- Local environments such as neighborhoods and cities
- Personal characteristics such as race, ethnicity, and nationality
- Learning histories such as family, social routines, customs, and experiences
- Language such as dialect and vocabulary (Center on PBIS, 2021e)

Hence, because PBIS must be adapted for cultural and contextual fit, it is not inherently culturally and linguistically responsive. Moreover, in reviewing the literature (Sugai et al., 2012; Vincent et al., 2015; Vincent & Tobin, 2011) about PBIS's limited effectiveness with underserved students, five key themes emerge. In effect, PBIS was:

1. Originally developed with students from the dominant culture in mind
2. Rooted in behaviorism, not sociocultural theory
3. Banked on an extrinsic rewards system
4. Focused on compliance rather than cooperation
5. Based on rigid rather than flexible procedures

These five main themes serve as rationales for supporting the case that PBIS is not authentically culturally and linguistically responsive and, therefore, needs to be made so to be effective with underserved students.

Originally Developed With Students From the Dominant Culture in Mind

Many practices and approaches that proliferate in U.S. public schools are touted as evidence based. In fact, being evidence or research based is considered a major requirement for adoption of new curricula and initiatives such as social-emotional learning (SEL) programs. All too often, though, the practices considered to be evidence based have a Eurocentric foundation with no representation of underserved cultures (Bal, 2018). This is also the case with PBIS.

In the late 1990s to early 2000s, when PBIS was initially being developed and vetted, it was primarily done using suburban schools with only students of the dominant culture (Bal, Thorius, & Kozleski, 2012). Essentially, this means that the original developers of PBIS established the effectiveness of PBIS practices primarily with White middle-class youth in mind, not with students of color nor those in urban environments.

From a CLR lens, this is problematic because CLR requires consideration of students' cultures in all practices. Furthermore, PBIS's framers originally conceptualized PBIS as being based on *universal* principles they perceived as "culturally neutral" and thus applicable in all cases (Cramer & Bennet, 2015; Johnson, Anhalt, & Cowan, 2018). Hence, because they founded PBIS on what they considered *universal* principles, the framers believed cultural differences of students were not a significant factor to consider, although they later shifted from this position (Johnson et al., 2018).

Again, this is in direct contrast to CLR, which is explicitly based on acknowledging the salience of cultural differences. Last, PBIS borrowed from the response to intervention (RTI) approach (Buffum, Mattos, & Malone, 2018), developed to support academic achievement, which also is not authentically culturally and linguistically responsive. According to Austin Buffum, Mike Mattos, and Janet Malone (2018):

> Traditionally, the RTI process is represented in the shape of a pyramid. The pyramid is commonly separated into tiers: Tier 1 represents core instruction, Tier 2 represents supplemental interventions, and Tier 3 represents intensive student supports. The pyramid is wide at the bottom to represent the instruction that all students receive. As students demonstrate the need for additional support, they receive increasingly more targeted and intensive help. (p. 2)

Research into the standard RTI framework reveals that RTI itself is lacking in "the recognition of culture and its role in learning" (Morales-James, Lopez, Wilkins, & Fergus, 2012).

Interestingly, from PBIS's inception, its developers recommended that PBIS be implemented with a *contextual fit*, but they provided few resources on how to do so and did not initially frame contextual fit in terms of cultural responsiveness (Vincent et al., 2015). In our work with schools and districts, this lack of communicating a transparent relationship between what they meant as contextual fit and cultural responsiveness understandably resulted in district and school officials not inherently considering cultural and linguistic responsiveness in developing and implementing their individual school's PBIS frameworks. The vast number of districts and schools implementing PBIS did so in a way that fit their environmental context, but they did not do so in alignment with the cultures of students from underserved backgrounds because PBIS was not originally conceived and communicated in this way.

As previously noted, though, PBIS's developers have since evolved from their original framing of contextual fit and now explicitly attempt to connect it with cultural responsiveness (Johnson et al., 2018; Sugai et al., 2012). Moreover, they, and others, expressly communicate the need for PBIS to be implemented in a culturally responsive manner to be optimally effective with underserved students and reduce racial disproportionality in exclusionary discipline (Bal et al., 2012; Parsons, 2018; Sugai et al., 2012).

Rooted in Behaviorism, Not Sociocultural Theory

When you think about the child development courses that you most likely took during your preparation to be an educator or at some point in your education career, names like B. F. Skinner, Jean Piaget, Lev Vygotsky, Albert Bandura, and others probably come to mind. However, you may not always make the direct connections between these scholars' theories and your instructional and behavior management practices. For instance, if you have used Lee Canter's (2010) assertive discipline approach in your classroom, have you ever stopped to think whether it is based on Skinner's operant conditioning theory or Bandura's social cognitive theory (Santrock, 2014)? Again, probably not, especially during your early years as a classroom teacher. More likely, you were in survival mode, trying to execute whatever behavior management approach you learned in your teacher preparation program or just using your prior ideas about discipline emanating from your years as a student and child on the receiving end of these practices. Yet, if you expect to have equitable experiences for your culturally and linguistically diverse students, it is critical that you take stock of whatever approach you have been utilizing in order to assess whether it is inherently culturally and linguistically responsive. This is the case with PBIS as well.

PBIS's roots are in behaviorism. The developers of PBIS acknowledge PBIS's behaviorist foundation and specifically state, "[PBIS] is rooted in the behavior analytic tradition" (Sugai et al., 2012, p. 200). And according to the Behavior Analyst Certification Board (2021), behaviorism is the primary theory underlying behavioral analysis. Introduced by Skinner, behaviorism is a theory that emphasizes behaviors of animal or human subjects could be changed through operant conditioning (Santrock, 2014). In other words, through the use of rewards and punishments, a subject, such as a student, can learn a desired behavior or stop an undesired behavior. This is evidenced in PBIS as teachers and staff praise students who follow behavioral expectations and reward them with tokens that they can trade for tangible prizes. It is also evidenced as teachers and staff give students negative consequences, such as loss of privileges and office discipline referrals, for not following behavioral expectations. PBIS's behaviorist roots are also exemplified in its focus on defining concrete and measurable outcomes. The behaviorist approach tends toward narrow explanations of human behavior, though, and therefore does not align with cultural and linguistic responsiveness.

Whereas PBIS is grounded in behaviorism, CLR is rooted in sociocultural theory. Sociocultural theory is credited to Lev Vygotsky, who argued about the role of culture and social interaction in learning (Santrock, 2014). According to John Santrock (2014), Vygotsky posited that human behavior is not merely a reaction to positive or negative stimuli; social interaction has a significant role in learning and development. Researchers Cheryl Utley, Elizabeth Kozleski, Anne Smith, and Ingrid Draper (2002) highlight this tension between PBIS's basis in behaviorism and CLR's basis in sociocultural theory in their explanation of the problem with PBIS's behaviorist roots. They explain that because a behaviorist approach does not consider the cultural traditions and ways of being of culturally and linguistically diverse students, as is inherent in the sociocultural tradition, this approach will reinforce the dominant culture's (or the White middle class's) beliefs about what are and are not appropriate behaviors. Therefore, educators will consistently evaluate culturally and linguistically diverse students' behaviors in relation to a culturally biased perspective, and they will provide rewards and consequences accordingly. Simply put, because behaviorism neglects to focus on cultural differences in determining whether a behavior is appropriate, it is not aligned with cultural and linguistic responsiveness.

Further spotlighting behaviorism's lack of consideration for culture and sociocultural theory's emphasis on the language of culture, Raymond Wlodkowski and Margery Ginsberg (1995) point out that in a culturally responsive approach, teachers support student behavior primarily through intrinsic motivation (for example, highlighting how the content of a lesson is relevant to students' lives) rather than extrinsic methods (for example, tangible rewards and negative consequences).

Banked on an Extrinsic Rewards System

Operant conditioning, or the use of extrinsic methods to reinforce desired behaviors, is a key element of the behaviorist tradition (McLeod, 2018) that is the theoretical basis for PBIS. According to the Center on PBIS (2021c), a key practice is educators' use of "procedures for encouraging expected behavior," which includes the use of extrinsic rewards. Specifically, it recommends the use of a token system as a tangible method for reinforcing desired behaviors. This system involves educators verbally acknowledging students for following schoolwide behavior expectations and giving them tokens that later can be traded for a prize. A Google search of the terms *PBIS* and *rewards* provides numerous web resources for teachers who are looking for extrinsic reward systems to use as a part of their PBIS approach.

Rooted in behaviorism, the systemic practice of giving students extrinsic rewards for complying with behavioral expectations is not culturally and linguistically responsive because it can create "cognitive dissonance for students who are confused about why adults would spend time setting up these kinds of reward structures when they are more familiar with approaches that teach through example, modeling, and story" (Kozleski, 2010, p. 5). That is to say the use of external rewards is not culturally congruent because culturally and linguistically diverse students may be typically accustomed to learning expected behaviors through explicit teaching and modeling rather than through tangible compensation. Moreover, the use of extrinsic rewards tends to prevent culturally and linguistically diverse students from being engaged and successful in school because of feelings of disconnect and coercion.

In contrast, from a CLR perspective, the use of intrinsic motivation is considered more effective than extrinsic rewards because it is more accommodating of cultural differences related to motivation (Ginsberg & Wlodkowski, 2019; Wlodkowski & Ginsberg, 1995). We are not saying that extrinsic rewards are ineffective or have no use (more on this in chapter 5, page 79), although Michael Ryan Hunsaker (2018), Kohn (2018), and others argue that external incentives are not effective and even detrimental. Rather, the key point is that PBIS's universal application of extrinsic rewards does not inherently align with CLR.

Focused on Compliance Rather Than Cooperation

Various classroom and schoolwide approaches to discipline, including the PBIS framework, emphasize getting students to comply with (or conform, acquiesce, or yield to) rules or behavioral expectations. Sugai and Horner (2002), two aforementioned originators of the PBIS framework, acknowledge that the first tier of PBIS (universal supports) has teachers reinforce student compliance with behavioral expectations.

Figure 2.1 illustrates the CLR undergirding (or four tiers of CLR prevention), which we term the *pre-tier* or *zero tier*, of PBIS. Ironically, PBIS uses the term *prevention* throughout all three of its tiers, while the zero tier of CLR is the positive assumption or belief that there will be no need for prevention.

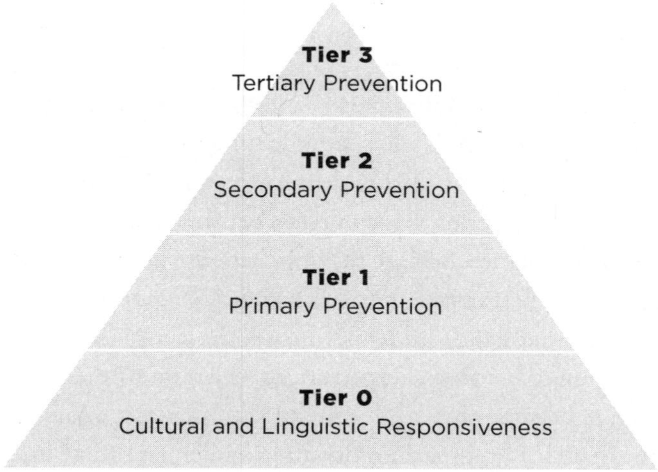

Tier 3
Tertiary Prevention

Tier 2
Secondary Prevention

Tier 1
Primary Prevention

Tier 0
Cultural and Linguistic Responsiveness

FIGURE 2.1: CLR-aligned PBIS tiers.

PBIS alignment with CLR then begins with the zero tier that requires the process described in chapter 1 (page 9). Table 2.1 (page 48) provides a more detailed description of the entire PBIS tiered prevention system, which is integral to PBIS.

Because PBIS focuses on enforcing acquiescence with behavioral expectations, though, it is not authentically culturally and linguistically responsive. In a CLR approach to discipline, rather than expecting students to merely obey rules, teachers inspire students to cooperate with school norms of acceptable behavior. On the surface, it may be difficult to tell the difference between a student who is choosing to cooperate and one who is

TABLE 2.1: PBIS Tiered Prevention System

Tier	Prevention Description
1. Primary (Universal)	Tier 1 supports serve as the foundation for behavior and academics. Schools provide these universal supports to all students. For most students, the core program gives them what they need to be successful and to prevent future problems.
2. Secondary (Targeted)	This level of support focuses on improving specific skill deficits students have. Schools often provide Tier 2 supports to groups of students with similar targeted needs. Providing support to a group of students provides more opportunities for practice and feedback while keeping the intervention maximally efficient. Students may need some assessment to identify whether they need this level of support and which skills to address. Tier 2 supports help students develop the skills they need to benefit core programs at the school.
3. Tertiary (Intensive)	Tier 3 supports are the most intensive supports the school offers. These supports are the most resource intensive due to the individualized approach of developing and carrying out interventions. At this level, schools typically rely on formal assessments to determine a student's need and to develop an individualized support plan. Student plans often include goals related to both academics as well as behavior support.

Source: Center on PBIS, 2021f.

merely complying with the rules. Both can appear to be on task or show positive interactions with peers, teachers, and staff. Underneath the surface, the story is different, though.

We can use Phillip Schlechty's (2011) delineation among levels of engagement to illustrate this difference. He explains that compliance involves low levels of commitment; students might be doing what teachers are making them do, but they are only complying because they either value the extrinsic rewards being offered or want to avoid negative consequences. On the other hand, students who are truly engaged have a high level of commitment. In relation to behavioral expectations, this commitment involves students choosing to cooperate because they find some type of intrinsic value and meaning in these expectations. In a CLR approach, motivating students to want to cooperate with norms of behavior is the name of the game.

PBIS's emphasis on compliance with behavioral expectations is even more troublesome because the expectations primarily reflect dominant culture norms (Wilson, 2015), and they often do not acknowledge the norms of culturally and linguistically diverse students. This means that culturally and linguistically diverse students are often expected to comply with behavioral norms that do not reflect what is valued in their home cultures, and this can have negative effects. Students may not feel validated, or they may feel like they are being forced to sell out their cultural identities in order to comply (Bal, 2018).

Moreover, because the PBIS framework does not inherently take into consideration that culture mediates all people's understanding and interpretation of the values that underlie behavioral expectations, the expectation of compliance with schoolwide norms creates conflicts for culturally and linguistically diverse students (Bal et al., 2012). For example, a common behavioral expectation in many schools using a PBIS framework is to *be respectful*. Respect, however, is a culturally mediated concept, and therefore subject to interpretation. Hence, it is problematic to expect culturally and linguistically diverse students, who have a different cultural conception of respect, to conform to the dominant culture's views about respect while their own view gets ignored or, worse, disparaged.

Instead of focusing on compliance, a CLR approach emphasizes inspiring students to cooperate with *collaboratively* developed, culturally resonant behavioral expectations (find out more on collaboration in chapter 5, page 79). Students cooperate with these *shared* expectations not because they are forced to but because they choose to follow them. Moreover, they choose to cooperate with the behavioral norms because they feel their own cultural beliefs are being validated and affirmed (Hollie, 2018). When culturally and linguistically diverse students can see how their cultural ways of doing and ways of being are both explicitly and implicitly valued, it develops a stronger connection among them and the classroom environment, teacher, and school setting. This stronger connection leads to a greater willingness and intrinsic desire to collaborate with the teacher's behavioral expectations.

Based on Rigid Rather Than Flexible Procedures

PBIS focuses on developing stable and rigid procedures or practices at each tier of a school's individualized PBIS system. The rigidity of these PBIS processes, such as PBIS's continuum of procedures for responding to challenging behaviors, is what makes PBIS not inherently culturally and linguistically responsive since CLR requires flexibility.

PBIS utilizes a three-tiered framework for preventing and intervening with challenging student behavior in a positive and nonpunitive manner. At the first tier, or the universal supports level, a hierarchy of consequences (a continuum of procedures for discouraging problem behaviors) that hold students responsible for "inappropriate" conduct is recommended by the Center on PBIS (2021c). Inherently, this fixed structure for holding students accountable for their choices is detrimental to culturally and linguistically diverse students.

Elizabeth Kozleski (2010), whose research focuses on equity and justice issues in inclusive education, specifically cautions educators against the use of inflexible systems or procedures with students of diverse backgrounds. She states:

> The rigidity of the system makes it difficult for students who need many experiences to be able to predict what may be expected and then act accordingly. And, because of the nature of the system and individual psychological and cultural patterns, the very system itself can create resistance and avoidance. (p. 5)

Many schools implementing PBIS, with whom we have worked, have a fixed system for identifying behaviors as *minor* or *major* behavioral issues or *problem* behaviors. In this system, teachers or a responding staff member should handle behaviors considered minor, and a school administrator (through an office referral) should handle behaviors considered major. Furthermore, teachers follow a prescribed procedure wherein they consider a student's exhibition of three minor behaviors as equivalent to a major behavior, and thus, they refer the student to the office. This lockstep adherence to procedure, though, does not give culturally and linguistically diverse students the opportunities and grace they need in order to learn how to adapt to behavioral expectations that often are culturally different. Additionally, this rigid system of applying negative consequences for minor and major behavioral issues is vulnerable to teachers' subjective judgments about the behaviors of culturally and linguistically diverse students, further exacerbating the impact of these inflexible systems. For example, conversational patterns vary from culture to culture. In some cultures, verbal overlap is the norm, whereas other cultures follow a turn-taking pattern. Therefore, if a teacher's cultural frame of reference is oriented toward turn-taking as socially acceptable, he or she may interpret verbal overlap as a negative behavior, and thus administer a consequence based on the rigid PBIS processes in place at the school.

Educators' subjective judgments about their underserved students' cultural behaviors are a key factor in the overrepresentation of Black, Indigenous, and Latinx students in exclusionary discipline, such as office disciplinary referrals and suspensions (Anyon et al., 2014; Bal, 2016; Eber, Upreti, & Rose, 2010; Parsons, 2018). Hence, it is critically important that procedures for addressing students' behaviors are flexible enough to take this into account.

As Kozleski (2010) notes, the rigidity of the PBIS systems can also cause culturally and linguistically diverse students to become resistant or avoidant. Resistance manifests as students refusing to cooperate or comply with expectations, avoiding activities, or even skipping classes or school altogether as a means of coping with inflexible procedures for responding to students' behaviors. Brenda Townsend (2000), for instance, notes that Black students often adopt these identity-preserving behaviors to counter implicit and explicit negative identity messages they receive due to disproportionate discipline that results from rigid and biased discipline systems. As previously noted, even when PBIS is implemented with fidelity, culturally and linguistically diverse students, particularly Black students, are still overrepresented in office discipline referrals, suspensions, and expulsions. Essentially, the use of a rigid system of consequences has not been effective due to culturally and linguistically diverse students' resistance to the very procedures intended to discourage "problem" behaviors.

In contrast, a CLR-aligned approach is more flexible because it involves inspiring students to want to cooperate with culturally congruent principles, rather than forcing them to conform to a rigid system. These principles serve as guides for expected behaviors that are situationally appropriate, instead of locking students into a preset system of rewards and consequences. For example, rather than following a continuum of consequences for rules violations, teachers using a CLR approach guide students to think about how they could better cooperate with shared principles of conduct and how they should be held accountable for not cooperating with shared behavioral expectations. Furthermore, instead of managing student behavior in a cookie-cutter fashion, teachers tailor positive acknowledgment and behavior accountability to each individual student's needs, similar to the logical consequences model promoted in Fay and Funk's (2016) love and logic approach. That is to say, in a CLR approach, teachers handle disciplinary situations on a fluid, case-by-case basis with the intent of helping students learn from the situations.

Conclusion

This chapter began with the question of whether PBIS is authentically culturally and linguistically responsive. The clear answer is *no*; PBIS was not originally intended to be culturally and linguistically responsive. Though we have made the case that PBIS is not authentically culturally and linguistically responsive, this framework is reassuringly compatible with cultural and linguistic responsiveness. You just need to intentionally and strategically align it to CLR. As noted, even the developers of PBIS acknowledge this in their own literature. Sugai and colleagues (2012) emphasize schools and districts need to ensure their PBIS frameworks have cultural and contextual fit, meaning they are culturally responsive.

Therefore, though PBIS is not inherently culturally and linguistically responsive, but could and should be so, the next question is, "How can schools make a PBIS framework authentically culturally and linguistically responsive?" We will answer that question in the second half of this book, but before that, we must explore why schools need an authentic culturally and linguistically responsive PBIS.

CHAPTER 3

The Need for Authentic Culturally and Linguistically Responsive PBIS

"THE CASE FOR AUTHENTICITY"
SHARROKY HOLLIE

The degree to which something is authentic is in the eye of the beholder, I suppose. I am frequently reminded of this when working with schools that believe they are being authentic in their cultural responsiveness only to find out that they are not. Prior to and during the COVID-19 pandemic, I worked with a school district in Texas whose staff were convinced that they were culturally responsive, or as they put it, "We have been doing this work for a while now." "This work," it turns out, was a series of professional development workshops, a couple of book studies, and an equity committee. They wanted me to visit, observe their great work, and offer suggestions for improvement.

To make a long story short, I told the staff that they had to step back and agree on how they were defining cultural responsiveness. They needed to aim for authenticity, not superficiality. They had to focus on the practice of CLR and use the learning (professional development, book studies, and such) as a means to an end. In other words, they had to be real about what CLR is and could be for them and also, what it couldn't.

The previous chapter provided the rationales for why PBIS, by its nature, is not culturally and linguistically responsive. These rationales are not a critique of PBIS. On the contrary, they are a call for creating CLR-aligned PBIS, whereby schools can have success with PBIS and CLR for all students, most importantly for the students who need that success the most.

To help educators fully understand and accept the need for CLR-aligned PBIS, we need to provide a deeper explanation of why it is necessary. This explanation is rooted in the idea that a deficit orientation is baked into the PBIS cake, oftentimes without anyone knowing it is there. In the work of equity generally, and CLR specifically, people can unintentionally undermine a goal while pursuing the goal's good intentions because the roots are already marred. Put another way, the thought that people are doing the right thing outweighs the fact that they may be going about it the wrong way. To make this point in the chapter, we will use another popular approach in schools—restorative justice practices—to explain the dynamic of "good intentions, poor execution." Then we will bring the dynamic back to PBIS by focusing on a case study that clearly explains why schools desperately need CLR-aligned PBIS.

The Success of Restorative Justice Practices

During our winter break in 2019, this headline flashed across the daily morning news feed: "Major new study finds restorative justice led to safer schools, but hurt black students' test scores" (Barnum, 2019). It caught our attention because restorative justice practices are a mainstay for many school districts as they face the challenges of disruptive behavior specifically and discipline in general. And it surprised us that a study found restorative justice practices work when implemented effectively. Throughout our work with schools across the United States, we have seen as many variations of restorative justice practices as we have seen schools and, for the most part, we have not seen successful models. Restorative justice consultant Joe Brummer (2016) concurs when he states despite clearly articulated descriptions and guiding principles, the implementation of restorative practices, like many school innovations, is incredibly uneven, with some schools having phenomenal success and others drowning in their own failure.

Rather than go on the article, we decided to read the study. The RAND Corporation, a research-based think tank, conducted the study mentioned in the news headline. The RAND website's description of the study states:

> This study of the implementation of restorative practices in the Pittsburgh Public Schools district (PPS) in school years 2015–16 and 2016–17 represents one of the first randomized controlled trials of the effects of restorative practices on classroom and school climates and suspension rates. . . . The authors examined a specific restorative practices program. The researchers found that PERC [Pursuing Equitable and Restorative Communities] achieved several positive effects, including an improvement in overall school climates (as rated by teachers), a reduction in overall suspension rates, and a reduction in the disparities in suspension rates between African American and white students and between low- and higher-income students. (Augustine et al., 2018)

Eureka! A result to celebrate. The news that teachers felt an overall improvement in school climate, that the average suspension rate was reduced, and, most significantly, that the suspension rates of African American students decreased showed restorative practices were worth the effort. This was the good news. But there was also the bad news that African American students' test scores suffered.

Before moving to the bad news, let's take a step back and better understand restorative practices. Castlebay Lane Charter Elementary School (n.d.) provides the following description of restorative practices:

> Restorative Justice is a philosophy and an approach to discipline that moves away from punishment toward restoring a sense of harmony and well-being for all those affected by a hurtful act. It provides families, schools, and communities a way to ensure accountability while at the same time breaking the cycle of retribution and violence. It is based on a view of resilience in children and youth and their capability to solve problems, as opposed to the youth themselves being the problems adults must fix.
>
> It focuses not on retribution but on reconnecting severed relationships and re-empowering individuals by holding them responsible. This approach acknowledges that, when a person does harm, it affects the persons they hurt, the community, and themselves.
>
> When using restorative practices, an attempt is made to repair the harm caused by one person to another and to the community so that everyone is moved toward healing.

The description fits the context of restorative justice practices specifically intended for schools, and speaks to possible reasons why the Pittsburgh schools found success (Augustine et al., 2018). On the surface, what is there not to like about restorative justice practices? Outside the challenges of deep implementation that many schools face, restorative justice practices almost sound too good to be true.

The Failure of Restorative Justice Practices

Here, then, is the bad news. Another finding of the RAND Corporation study turned out to be even more newsworthy than the success of restorative justice practices (Augustine et al., 2018). The second part of the headline we read noted that Black students' test scores were negatively affected by restorative practice. Not only did their academic scores not improve, they worsened. In the article, Matt Barnum (2019) states:

> While restorative [justice practices] didn't have a significant effect on reading scores, math scores for students in grades 3 through 8 did fall significantly. The impact was not felt equally: It was black students, not white students, whose scores fell. A black student at the 50th percentile would have dropped to roughly the 44th percentile as a result of the initiative.

For us, the cause of the academic setback was immediately obvious. Suspending students has become an instructional intervention for most schools, whether it be in-school or out-of-school suspensions. Understated in the controversy of historical disproportionality in suspensions and expulsions is the notion that not having to deal with suspended and expelled students was often a means to an unintentional end, which was that teachers had no need to teach "those students" because they were not in school.

The results of the RAND study (Augustine et al., 2018) imply that with reduced suspensions came increased numbers of students in class who now had to be taught. But teachers could not teach them in the same way as before because that way had probably led many of them to discipline struggles in the first place, which then escalated into disruptive behavior or even worse over time. Something was missing before suspensions and after restoration: teachers needed to instruct these students in a culturally and linguistically responsive way (Hollie, 2018). Yes, restorative justice practices worked to some extent, but the question became this: What do schools do once "those students" are back in the classroom? Hence, the need for CLR.

Deficit Origins of Restorative Justice Practices

Unbeknownst to many, restorative justice practices originate from penitentiary institutions. According to the International Institute for Restorative Practices (n.d.):

> In the modern context, restorative justice originated in the 1970s as mediation or reconciliation between victims and offenders. In 1974 Mark Yantzi, a probation officer, arranged for two teenagers to meet directly with their victims following a vandalism spree and agree to restitution. The positive response by the victims led to the first victim-offender reconciliation program, in Kitchener, Ontario, Canada, with the support of the Mennonite Central Committee and collaboration with the local probation department (McCold, 1999; Peachey, 1989). The concept subsequently acquired various names, such as victim-offender mediation and victim-offender dialogue, as it spread through North America and to Europe through the 1980s and 1990s (Umbreit & Greenwood, 2000).

So, over time, a practice that started with victims and offenders has ended up in classrooms across the United States. To accept the premise of restorative justice practices, one must accept that these practices first emanated from a punitive place. In other words, the penal aspect of these practices makes them deficit oriented on general principle. For students, beginning with restoration is certainly not a place of leverage for empowerment. Common synonyms for *restore* are *reinstate*, *replace*, *reimpose*, *rehabilitate*, and *re-establish*. These words indicate something is wrong in the first place—a hallmark of deficit thinking. PBIS originates from a subtle deficit premise as well.

In chapter 2, Table 2.1 (page 48) discusses the PBIS tiers as preventative measures. We interpret the concept of prevention as deficit here, simply based on what teachers are trying to prevent—problematic behavior as the starting point. What do people want to prevent, collectively? Crime. Disease. Climate change. In the case of PBIS, people want to prevent new cases of problem behaviors. We interpret *prevention* in PBIS as a sugar-coated word for negative assumptions about student behaviors. Tier 1 in PBIS automatically assumes there will be behavior that teachers need to prevent or correct. CLR fundamentally challenges this assumption of prevention around some students' behaviors by viewing the behaviors as misunderstood culturally and linguistically and then presumes that prevention, as a concept, is not necessary when the behavior is cultural. Recall the Three Column activity from chapter 1 (page 33), which provides a process for determining which behaviors are cultural and which behaviors are unacceptable.

Tiers 2 and 3 only worsen the deficit thinking because they are supposed to reduce behaviors that teachers should have prevented in the first place. This is a slippery slope, not only for PBIS in its inherent deficit orientation but also, more strikingly, for students. The whole point of cultural responsiveness is to validate and affirm those cultural and linguistic behaviors that institutions, including schools, invalidate and disaffirm from the start. Unintentionally, PBIS perpetuates this institutional bias by beginning with problem behaviors and not students' cultural and linguistic assets. To bring the point home, we will examine examples taken right out of the *PBIS Cultural Responsiveness Field Guide* (Leverson et al., 2019).

Examples of Institutional Bias From the PBIS Cultural Responsiveness Field Guide

No other source makes the points of deficit origination and good intentions better than the *PBIS Cultural Responsiveness Field Guide: Resources for Trainers and Coaches* (Leverson et al., 2019). The stated purpose of the field guide is as follows:

> This field guide outlines an integrated framework to embed equity efforts into school-wide positive behavioral interventions and supports (SWPBIS) by aligning culturally responsive practices to the core components of SWPBIS. The goal of using this guide is to make school systems more responsive to the cultures and communities that they serve. (Leverson et al., 2019, p. 1)

This is the clearest attempt that we have seen to align PBIS with cultural responsiveness, yet it still misses the mark by demonstrating the lack of the essentials of CLR as a specific brand, which validates and affirms cultural and linguistic behaviors. In the *PBIS Cultural Responsiveness Field Guide*, cultural responsiveness includes the following five core components.

1. Identity
2. Voice
3. Supportive environment
4. Situational appropriateness
5. Data for equity

We are going to focus on core component 4, *situational appropriateness*, because it is directly lifted from the CLR research and approach that we espouse (Hollie, 2018). While the field guide uses the terminology of CLR, it misses the cultural and linguistic significance of the approach. A comparison of Hollie's (2018) and the field guide's definitions for situational appropriateness shows the difference.

Hollie (2018) defines *situational appropriateness* as "the concept of determining what is the most appropriate cultural and linguistic behavior for the situation *without giving up one's culture and language*" (p. 52). The field guide's authors define *situational appropriateness* in this way: "Situational appropriateness is the ability to determine what types of behavior will ensure positive outcomes in a given setting and demonstrate those skills with fluency. Situational appropriateness also includes altering one's behaviors when settings, contexts, or companions change" (Leverson et al., 2019, p. 27). Although on the surface the definitions are similar, a deeper examination explicitly and implicitly reveals they are significantly different. One difference is the former definition is not tied to a value or measure, such as "positive outcomes" or "skills with fluency." A second and more important distinction is the last phrase of Hollie's (2018) definition, which explicitly states "without giving up one's culture and language." What the field guide does *not* say is that students should not have to feel in any way that their behaviors are negative, wrong, or unaccepted. By using terms like *positive*, the inverse automatically becomes negative, and therein lies the problem with PBIS.

The field guide's authors (Leverson et al., 2019) reference Hollie's book (2018), including exact words and concepts, but misconstrue them to fit the PBIS framework. Let us emphatically say that we do not believe the field guide's authors intentionally twist Hollie's words and perspective. In this case, we believe that there is a simple lack of depth and clarity around how Hollie (2018) defines CLR and situational appropriateness. Beyond the definition discrepancy, the field guide includes several examples that reflect the interplay between good intentions and poor execution; the following sections demonstrate two such examples.

Example A

In appendix I of the field guide (Leverson et al., 2019), the authors directly quote Hollie's (2018) concept of VABB, or "validation, affirmation, building, and bridging" (p. 47). Before analyzing the authors' definition of VABB, let's recap our definition from chapter 1 (page 13): to *validate and affirm* means to make legitimate and positive the cultural and linguistic behaviors of historically marginalized populations that mainstream media, social media, institutions, and research have made illegitimate and negative. Schools, as institutions, have to do three things to validate and affirm: (1) talk to students differently, meaning no punitive, negative, or consequential talk as it applies to cultural and linguistic behaviors; (2) relate to students differently by building on the cultural assets the students bring to school rather than so-called liabilities; and (3) teach differently, which includes using instructional activities that validate and affirm students. To *build and bridge* simply means to access students' cultural assets and use these assets to bridge students to academic and social success.

To its credit, the definition in the *PBIS Cultural Responsiveness Field Guide* (Leverson et al., 2019) closely matches what we previously described, but it is a case of *so close, yet so far* as it applies to cultural responsiveness. For example, here is the field guide's definition of *validation*:

> Validation is legitimizing aspects of students' cultures that have historically been seen as illegitimate by the dominant culture, including intentionally allowing time and space for cultural aspects within the school day. These cultural aspects include language, teachings, and rites of passage. (Leverson et al., 2019, p. 47)

Close enough, one might say. But here is the example of culture provided right after that definition:

> Rap music, for example, sometimes has a negative connotation in dominant society due to language or themes. However, rap music can also be seen as an effective form of communication that requires creativity and spontaneity. Strategies for validation include displaying aspects of students' culture in the classroom and around the school, asking students to share their experiences, and listening non-judgmentally. (Leverson et al., 2019, p. 47)

Surprisingly, rap music is the first and only example of a cultural behavior that this field guide provides as needing to be validated and affirmed, which proves the laden deficit perspective and also hemorrhages a classic negative stereotype linking rap music to specific cultural behaviors. Why not list heavy metal too? The CLR focus on cultural behaviors is more specific and comprehensive, as demonstrated in the section, Commonly Misunderstood Cultural and Linguistic Behaviors, in chapter 1 (page 29).

The *PBIS Cultural Responsiveness Field Guide*'s definition of *affirmation* is "explicitly acknowledging the worth of students' cultures and learning histories" (Leverson et al., 2019, p. 47). But again, the field guide uses rap music as the only identifier of a cultural behavior: "If rap music is an aspect of student culture at a school, affirmation requires harnessing and capitalizing on the communication, creativity, and spontaneity of the music" (Leverson et al., 2019, p. 47). In an authentic culturally and linguistically responsive sense, affirmation has more to do with images of marginalized cultures and languages in print and electronic media than with specific cultural behaviors (Hollie, 2018). To affirm students, schools must proactively present images and select textbooks that ensure authentic, original representations of diverse students are available. The PBIS definition of culture in this example is too narrow, and ironically, the use of rap music as an example speaks to the exact generalizations that CLR tries to avoid.

Example B

Many words used throughout the *PBIS Cultural Responsiveness Field Guide* (Leverson et al., 2019) point toward implicit deficit thinking and are therefore strongly discouraged within an authentic CLR framework. Consistent with the pattern of good intentions, poor execution, these terms sound good on the surface, but they also make a judgment that does not align with the CLR mindset. For CLR, the general principle is to avoid words that are value based or judgmental in nature, or that portend any type of right-or-wrong dynamic. Following is a list of deficit terms found throughout the *PBIS Cultural Responsiveness Field Guide* (Leverson et al., 2019).

- Respect(ful)
- Corrections
- Formal
- Insulting
- Aggressive
- Regulate
- Code switch
- Unwanted
- Wrong
- Maintain

Deficit statements found in the field guide include the following (Leverson et al., 2019).

- Sit quietly when on the floor.
- Zero talking while the teacher is reading.
- Line up quietly.
- Stay in your own spaces.

Many of these terms and statements appear to be positive and supportive, but when viewed through the lens of authentic cultural responsiveness, they come across differently. For example, the terms *respect*, *respectful*, and *respectfully* appear in almost all PBIS materials we have ever seen. On the surface, the term *respect* might not seem questionable. Let us look more closely at this term.

First, *respect* is a relative term, especially in regard to culture. What is respectful in one person's culture may be different in another person's culture. A common example of a cultural difference around respect is the element of eye contact. In some cultures, maintaining eye contact is respectful, while in other cultures, maintaining that same eye contact is disrespectful. The point is it all depends. Thus, when teachers tell students to "be respectful," like in PBIS, questions arise around whose respect and the relativity of respect.

Second, a deep dive into the word *respect* shows that its root meaning is to look back on or look back with perspective. Respect is essentially an observation, which means if one used it as originally intended, then respect would fit with cultural responsiveness. The relativity of culture would fit into the notion of looking back with perspective. But the way PBIS and society in general use the word *respect*, it means to behave the way other people think one should behave, and when one does not, the behavior is deemed disrespectful. Steve Pavlina (2014), an expert in conscious growth, which is based on self-help and care literature, states:

> Respect is very much an "eye of the beholder" concept. What one person sees as respectful could be interpreted as disrespectful by another, and vice versa. So if someone behaves as you believe people should behave, that's a show of respect. If someone violates your expectations in ways you dislike, you may interpret that as a sign of disrespect. And from your perspective, you'd always be right.

For this reason, the term *respect* does not mesh with cultural responsiveness and could be considered negative, depending on the cultural perspective.

Another example in which the intent does not match the actions in PBIS is with phrases like *zero talking while the teacher is reading*. This edict negates a common cultural behavior—which, ironically, the field guide acknowledges—and that is verbal overlap. In some cultures (languages), talking while someone else is talking, or overlapping, is a positive norm because it shows engagement and interest in what the person is saying. In school culture, however, verbal overlap is typically seen as disrespectful, which leads to a PBIS statement like *no talking while the teacher is reading*.

If PBIS were authentic in its cultural responsiveness, then it would acknowledge the fact that students will have opportunities to verbally overlap while the teacher is reading, depending on the situation. This will depend on the type of talking, the content of the comment, and the timing. For example, it would not be situationally appropriate to conduct a full-blown conversation during the reading, much as it would not be appropriate to have a full-blown conversation during a movie; students might instead briefly talk about the movie during the movie. The inauthentic version of CLR wants it both ways— acknowledging the cultural behavior but then having a rule regarding when the behavior is and is not appropriate. In CLR, it cannot be both ways, which is why PBIS needs CLR.

Conclusion

In summary, schools must authentically align PBIS with cultural responsiveness. This chapter described why they need this alignment. Teachers must match the good intentions of PBIS with great execution; this requires that they understand and acknowledge

PBIS's inherent deficit orientation. In order to help schools get on the right foot, we must explicitly state that they have been on the wrong foot, albeit unintentionally. They need a better understanding of the core philosophy and principles of CLR, and not cursory or cliché uses of key CLR terms and concepts, like in the *PBIS Cultural Responsiveness Field Guide* (Leverson et al., 2019). Finally, their use of deficit language must change to reflect the relativity and authenticity of culture in relation to situational appropriateness versus a set of arbitrary rules and expectations.

This chapter concludes part 1, the *why*, which started with an explanation of the basics of culturally responsive classroom management. It also included the rationale for why PBIS is not inherently culturally responsive by providing five arguments based on PBIS research and literature. The first part concluded with a demonstration of the need for CLR-aligned PBIS that is clearly not deficit oriented in its function or in its use of language. CLR-aligned PBIS hits the bull's-eye of the target, not just the target.

The *How* of Culturally and Linguistically Responsive PBIS

Part 2, the *how*, delineates what is required to hit that bull's-eye of culturally and linguistically responsive PBIS. Chapter 4 provides three simple but complex steps to apply a CLR lens to PBIS; chapter 5 puts the CLR concept of situational appropriateness in the context of PBIS; and chapter 6 specifies students' perspective and the ways that CLR-aligned PBIS applies to their school experience.

CHAPTER 4

CLR-PBIS Alignment, Assessment, and Activation

"A QUESTION OF EQUITY"
SHARROKY HOLLIE

Of the many lessons that have come out of the 2020 COVID-19 pandemic and the ongoing racial justice reckoning, one that has stuck with me is that schools are in desperate need of not only what to do but how to do the work of equity and cultural responsiveness. I can remember being in numerous Zoom meetings with schools that simply did not know what they were supposed to do to be equitable. Prior to the pandemic and the summer of protests that followed the murder of George Floyd, most people understood that they had to do more. Thinking you are equitable versus actually being equitable are two different things. One district in Texas expressed dire concerns about its long-standing implementation of PBIS, almost ten years, but very little had changed in terms of resolving the inequities with its African American students and discipline. I could see the frustration in their faces, virtually. The unspoken question on their faces was, "How do we do this?"

The Texas administrators in this story represent the audience for part 2 of this book. Frankly, when it comes to the work of equity and cultural responsiveness, we feel there has been too much talk and not enough action. In our work with school districts, there is a strong desire to be equitable and culturally responsive with PBIS; they are just looking for how to do it. This chapter begins that focus—the *how*.

This chapter is divided into what will first appear as three seemingly simple steps: (1) alignment, (2) assessment, and (3) activation. But the three steps, upon closer look, are complex because they call for deep reflections about actual practices and honest discussions about matters related to the infrastructure of schools and districts, such as leadership capacity, resource allocation, and time allowance for professional development.

Alignment

Common interpretations of the word *alignment* do not capture all that this step entails. To illustrate the complexity of alignment, let's first define it in automotive maintenance terms. A wheel alignment is "an adjustment of a vehicle's suspension—the system that connects a vehicle to its wheels. It is not an adjustment of the tires or wheels themselves," which most laypeople think (Bridgestone Tire, n.d.). "The key to proper alignment is adjusting the angles of the tires," which affects how the tires make contact with the road (Bridgestone Tire, n.d.). Simply put, a true alignment involves more than just straightening things out. Therefore, aligning PBIS to CLR will not just be a quick and simple adjustment. CLR is, in effect, the school's suspension (no pun intended), and PBIS is the tires contacting the road. In a school, CLR should in effect infuse the entire school (the system), including other programs, like social-emotional learning, trauma-informed instruction, restorative practices, and, yes, PBIS.

Alignment of PBIS to CLR ensures that the three integral aspects of culturally and linguistically responsive PBIS discussed in chapter 1 (page 9) are actively in place. As a review of those aspects, and also as a means of reflection, you must address these three questions.

1. To what extent are you following or implementing the core principles of CLR?
2. To what degree have you reflected on a schoolwide classroom management system, if one exists in the first place?
3. With what level of intensity and frequency have your staff discussed the acceptance, validation, and affirmation of your students' cultural and linguistic behaviors that have garnered different disciplinary perspectives or actions?

These three reflective questions undergird (or suspend, to stick with the car analogy) the PBIS framework. Without the CLR connection, PBIS and other initiatives have the potential to not be as effective as they can be.

PBIS alignment with CLR then begins with the zero tier (or undergirding), as described in chapter 2 (see figure 2.1, page 47, and table 2.1, page 48) and requires the steps described in chapter 1 (page 9) for establishing an effective classroom management system. Following are the four steps for aligning CLR to PBIS, for the purpose of reflecting on your alignment.

1. Apply the core principles of CLR with authenticity.

2. Determine whether the behavior in question is a cultural behavior or an unacceptable behavior. With the CLR mindset, teachers give students the benefit of the doubt that their behaviors are cultural but not always contextually appropriate. Plain and simple, in most cases, students do not intentionally behave in so-called disrespectful or disruptive ways. In the pre-tier (zero tier), teachers consider the high probability that cultural misunderstandings at play get turned into discipline issues.

3. If the behavior is cultural, then teachers must apply the schoolwide commitment to validation and affirmation (the CLR skill set).

4. If teachers determine the behavior is unacceptable, then the PBIS process of intervention (versus prevention) begins, meaning the first tier becomes applicable.

CLR still can have some influence in tiers 1 and 2, but the thought is if the situation is tier 3, then the given interventions and supports become more important. Note that CLR is not a panacea or magic bullet. You should look at your tier 1 school- and classroom-wide systems with a CLR lens, which hearkens back to chapter 1's (page 9) focus on having an effective classroom management system congruent with CLR. Tier 2, while focused on specialized groups of students placed at risk for behavioral challenges, can still be an opportunity to include a CLR perspective, but in limited ways. CLR is an eliminator, meaning that it will eliminate situations where oftentimes schools falsely label students as having behavioral problems when, in fact, they would benefit more from validation and affirmation than from consequences and modifications. The pre-tier eliminates many students from potentially being wrongly placed in tier 1. In tier 2, schools should use CLR to guarantee that the students placed at risk for behavioral challenges have not been falsely labeled. In this way, schools can have more confidence that if the situation rises to tier 3, then it has a very low probability of being culturally or linguistically related.

Aligning PBIS to CLR starts with a reflection on your school staff's CLR buy-in, levels of implementation, and evidenced impact. Next, your school must look at CLR as an undergirding to the PBIS system and consider to what extent the school has validated and affirmed cultural and linguistic behaviors so it can make connections to perceived behavioral issues. Last, your school must apply CLR to tiers 1 and 2 as a means to avoid pushing students through the system who should not be there because their behaviors are cultural (not wrong or bad), and teachers should validate and affirm those behaviors. After the school aligns PBIS to CLR, then it must assess the fidelity of PBIS implementation.

Assessment

To ensure that your school's PBIS framework is aligned with CLR, the tools you use for assessing fidelity of PBIS implementation must also be comprehensively aligned with CLR. This involves examining all aspects of PBIS—systems, practices, and data for all tiers—for CLR infusion. When it comes to assessing the fidelity of standard PBIS framework implementation (without CLR), the Center on PBIS (2021a) has various tools to assist schools with gauging how accurately the core components of PBIS are being put into action.

A search of the center's website (www.pbis.org) turns up multiple resources that schools can utilize for this purpose. Preeminent among them is the SWPBIS Tiered Fidelity Inventory. According to the Center on PBIS (2021a), the purpose of the Tiered Fidelity Inventory is "to provide a valid, reliable, and efficient measure of the extent to which school personnel are applying the core features of school-wide positive behavioral interventions and supports (SWPBIS)." Schools can use this assessment to examine the implementation of all three tiers of PBIS's multitiered framework.

Used in conjunction with the inventory is the Tiered Fidelity Inventory Walkthrough Tool. According to Robert Algozzine and colleagues (2014), the Tiered Fidelity Inventory Walkthrough Tool is "an interview form used for the tier 1 scale that includes questions for randomly selected staff and students" (p. 5). Someone external to the school can use this tool for evaluating fidelity of implementation, or a member of a school's PBIS leadership team can use it to monitor the progress of PBIS implementation (Algozzine et al., 2014). In our encounters with schools using PBIS, we have found the use of the Tiered Fidelity Inventory and the Walkthrough Tool to be ubiquitous.

Despite the widespread use of the SWPBIS Tiered Fidelity Inventory and Tiered Fidelity Inventory Walkthrough Tool by many schools, neither fidelity assessment tool is aligned with CLR and therefore they need to be supplemented. In response to this, Leverson and colleagues (2019) developed the *Tiered Fidelity Inventory Cultural Responsiveness Companion* to be used in conjunction with, but not replace, the Tiered Fidelity Inventory. Additionally, they created the Modified Tiered Fidelity Inventory Walkthrough Tool to use in place of the standard PBIS Tiered Fidelity Inventory Walkthrough Tool. Both of these assessment instruments are intended to help identify how to improve culturally responsive PBIS implementation. Leverson and colleagues (2019) recommend that school PBIS leadership teams use the Midwest PBIS Network's (2015) *Culturally Responsive School-Wide PBIS Team Self-Assessment, Version 3.0* to assist them in tracking their progress toward enhancing cultural responsiveness. According to the Midwest PBIS Network (2015), school leadership teams should use this tool annually to address the core components of PBIS—such as systems, practices, and data—across all three tiers.

Systems refers to how the different aspects of your school's PBIS framework work together as a whole in service of your school's intended outcomes. *Practices* refers to PBIS operations that must be customary or, in other words, accepted as routine. Finally, *data* refers to the evidence that school leadership teams need to regularly collect and analyze in order to inform decision making.

To be clear, these tools are comprehensive and strongly emphasize the need to implement PBIS in a culturally responsive manner. The Midwest PBIS Network (2015) explicitly notes the need "to ensure that School-wide Positive Behavior Interventions and Supports (SWPBIS) practices and systems have equal impact for *all* [emphasis added] students" (p. 1). Moreover, the *Culturally Responsive School-Wide PBIS Team Self-Assessment, Version 3.0* (Midwest PBIS Network, 2015) covers many key elements of assessing PBIS fidelity for alignment with cultural responsiveness. With their tool, Leverson and colleagues (2019) even assert that "SWPBIS is not fully implemented until it is culturally responsive" (p. 2). But as noted previously, although these authors aligned their PBIS fidelity assessment tool with CLR, they unintentionally misconstrued how to assess PBIS for CLR in some aspects of their *Tiered Fidelity Inventory Cultural Responsiveness Companion.*

If you have extensive experience with the standard PBIS Tiered Fidelity Inventory, then you know that an assessment of implementation fidelity involves examining each core component of PBIS across all three tiers (universal, targeted, and intensive). Therefore, knowing how to assess PBIS implementation fidelity aligned with CLR across each tier is critical. In assessing the fidelity of culturally and linguistically responsive PBIS, you must acknowledge that these tools overlap and parallel each other. They have commonalities because they align to the standard PBIS framework and general characteristics of cultural responsiveness. Again, though, what follows is differentiated by what we feel is a more accurate and complete alignment of PBIS with CLR.

As noted earlier, aligning PBIS to CLR is not a simple fix; it requires adjusting the entire PBIS framework. Moreover, CLR is positioned as a pre-tier or zero tier on which all the other tiers of PBIS must be built. That being said, it is critical that tier 1 systems, practices, and data are solidly in place since tiers 2 and 3 build on tier 1. Tiers 2 and 3 must be held up by a structurally sound tier 1 that thoroughly aligns with cultural and linguistic responsiveness. This is particularly essential because, according to the Center on PBIS (2021b), tier 1 systems, practices, and data have an impact on *all* students across *all* settings; this is why they are referred to as universal supports. Following that, tier 2 is geared toward some (but not all) students, while tier 3 is more focused on a few (see figure 2.1, page 47, and table 2.1, page 48).

The assessment tool in the following three sections is designed to help you assess systems, practices, and data in all three tiers of your school's PBIS framework for CLR alignment. We developed this tool after first evaluating the strengths and needs of the previously described PBIS implementation assessment tools with a CLR lens. We then looked at all the key systems, practices, and data at each PBIS tier, as described by the Center on PBIS (2021a, b, c, d, e, and f) on its official website (www.pbis.org) and the SWPBIS Tiered Fidelity Inventory version 2.1 (Algozzine et al., 2019) to develop our own PBIS fidelity assessment tool that is comprehensively aligned to cultural and linguistic responsiveness. Our intention is to provide educators with the most culturally and linguistically accurate tool for assessing PBIS implementation fidelity.

The following section focuses on how to assess PBIS implementation more accurately for CLR alignment.

Assessment of Tier 1 Systems, Practices, and Data

The CLR-PBIS Fidelity Assessment Tool in figure 4.1 focuses on tier 1 assessment. The plain font details the standard PBIS systems as described on the OSEP Technical Assistance Center on PBIS website (www.pbis.org), while the bold font delineates CLR alignment for each PBIS system, practice, or data source. Use this tool to reflect on your school's PBIS framework.

Assessment of Tier 2 Systems, Practices, and Data

Now that you have used the CLR-PBIS Fidelity Assessment Tool in figure 4.1 to review how to assess tier 1 systems, practices, and data for CLR alignment, it's time to turn to tier 2. As previously explained, the purpose of tier 2 is to provide targeted support to *some* students (up to approximately 15 percent) for whom tier 1 supports are not working and who need additional supports to prevent more challenging behaviors from manifesting. Optimally, the percentage of students requiring targeted support will be even less if tier 1 supports are truly aligned to CLR. Also, it is essential that educators not merely look at what they can do at the tier 2 level to improve students' behaviors. PBIS teams that are CLR must be willing and able to critically analyze their school's tier 2 systems, practices, and data to identify changes they need to make to better support students. In other words, rather than placing the responsibility for change on students (or their parents, for that matter), CLR-PBIS teams take on the responsibility to modify or adapt the systems, practices, and data to be culturally and linguistically responsive (Leverson et al., 2019).

The CLR-PBIS Fidelity Assessment Tool in figure 4.2 (page 73) is designed to assess tier 2 of your PBIS framework for alignment with CLR. The plain font details the standard PBIS systems as described on the OSEP Technical Assistance Center on PBIS website (www.pbis.org), while the bold font delineates CLR alignment for each PBIS system, practice, or data source.

0—Not Implemented; 1—Partially Implemented; 2—Mostly Implemented; 3—Fully Implemented				
Systems	**0**	**1**	**2**	**3**
There is an established **CLR-PBIS** leadership team **that is diverse and authentically inclusive of students, parents, and community members of underserved groups**.				
All school personnel on the CLR-PBIS team have training in CLR.				
Regular meetings are held **at times that accommodate the schedules of underserved groups**.				
The school has a commitment statement for establishing a positive schoolwide social culture **that is inclusive of language recognizing inequities and the need for validating, affirming, building, and bridging underserved students**.				
There is ongoing use of data for decision making **to identify and address inequities in disciplinary and academic outcomes**.				
Professional development plans **include comprehensive and ongoing training for all personnel in CLR**.				
There is a personnel evaluation plan **that includes the expectation that all personnel have a foundation in CLR and adhere to equitable practices; hiring criteria use CLR as a lens**.				
The office discipline referral process requires personnel to first determine whether a student's behavior is cultural as well as consider other factors relevant to the student's behavior (for example, special education status, relationship to adverse childhood experiences, and so on).				
The three Ds (defiance, disrespect, and disruption) are removed from office discipline referral forms.				
Practices	**0**	**1**	**2**	**3**
The school has three to five schoolwide positive expectations and behaviors **that are CLR**.				
The school's **CLR** schoolwide positive expectations and behaviors are defined **collaboratively with the CLR-PBIS leadership team using a CLR lens**.				
The school's **CLR** schoolwide positive expectations and behaviors are taught **using CLR instructional strategies with a structured method for communicating behavioral expectations**.				
The concept of situational appropriateness is taught and used to frame cultural behaviors in terms of situational appropriateness as opposed to "problem" behaviors.				

FIGURE 4.1: CLR-PBIS Fidelity Assessment Tool—tier 1 (universal supports).

continued →

Practices	O	1	2	3
There are established **CLR** classroom expectations aligned with **CLR** schoolwide expectations.				
CLR procedures for encouraging expected behaviors **(for example, specific positive feedback, a 5:1 ratio of positive interactions, regular celebrations and acknowledgment ceremonies, and positive intermittent reinforcement) are collaboratively selected by the CLR-PBIS leadership team and utilized by all personnel**.				
CLR procedures for discouraging "problem" behavior are **used in a flexible, context-specific manner (for example, logical consequences) as opposed to as a rigid hierarchy of consequences**.				
"Problem" behaviors are defined using a CLR lens in which cultural behaviors are clearly identified and separated from universally unacceptable ones.				
Cross-culturally unacceptable behaviors are clearly categorized as staff managed (minor) versus office managed (major).				
Cultural behaviors are addressed using the VABB framework (validated, affirmed, built, and bridged).				
CLR restorative practices are used to address cross-culturally unacceptable behaviors.				
CLR procedures for encouraging school-family partnerships are **established by the CLR-PBIS leadership team and utilized by teachers, administrators, and other pertinent staff**.				
Teachers regularly use CLR instructional and engagement practices that are intended to validate and affirm cultural behaviors and juxtaposed with those intended to build and bridge students to school cultural behaviors.				
Data	**O**	**1**	**2**	**3**
Data are regularly collected and analyzed **for signs of disproportionality in discipline, especially based on racial or ethnic demographics; intersectionality with special education status, sexual orientation, gender identification, sex, and socioeconomic status is also considered**.				
There is some type of schoolwide information system for collecting discipline and academic data about students **where the data can be disaggregated by different demographic subgroups, staff making office referrals, time, setting, and behavior**.				
The Tiered Fidelity Inventory is used to assess how closely personnel apply the core features of PBIS **in combination with (or replaced by) this CLR-PBIS Fidelity Assessment Tool**.				

Source: Adapted from Center on PBIS, 2021c.

*Visit **go.SolutionTree.com/diversityandequity** for a free reproducible version of this figure.*

0—Not Implemented; 1—Partially Implemented; 2—Mostly Implemented; 3—Fully Implemented				
Systems	**0**	**1**	**2**	**3**
There is an intervention team (tier 2 team) with a coordinator **who is trained in CLR and understands cultural behaviors**.				
The intervention team (tier 2 team) members and coordinator have behavioral expertise **that includes CLR, CLR-SEL, and an understanding of healing-centered engagement (trauma-sensitive schooling)**.				
Fidelity and outcome data are collected **and analyzed for signs of disproportionality**.				
There is a **CLR** screening process to identify students needing tier 2 support **so underserved students are not misidentified or overidentified**.				
The intervention team members and coordinator have access to training and technical assistance, **especially in CLR practices (for example, CLR functional behavioral assessments [FBAs])**.				
Administrators have a process for identifying groups of personnel who may require more targeted support in CLR (for example, teachers who are identified as persistently referring students to the office in a racially disproportionate way).				
Practices	**0**	**1**	**2**	**3**
Students receive increased instruction and practice with self-regulation and social skills **done in a culturally and linguistically responsive manner and aligned with healing-centered engagement practices (for example, CLR trauma-informed practices)**.				
Students receive increased adult supervision by staff **who have an understanding of the differences between cultural behaviors and universally unacceptable behaviors**.				
Students receive increased opportunities for positive reinforcement **delivered by staff in a culturally and linguistically responsive manner in which cultural behaviors are also validated and affirmed**.				
Students receive increased precorrections that **staff implement in a culturally and linguistically responsive manner with an understanding of the differences between cultural behaviors and universally unacceptable behaviors and how to utilize the VABB framework with cultural behaviors**.				

FIGURE 4.2: CLR-PBIS Fidelity Assessment Tool—tier 2 (targeted supports).

continued →

Practices	0	1	2	3
There is an increased focus on the possible function of **"problem" behaviors with an examination of personnel practices (for example, traditional teaching strategies, racial or cultural microaggressions, and punitive practices) that may not be culturally and linguistically responsive and therefore may be antecedents to the "problem" behaviors. The possibilities of externalizations and internalizations due to adverse childhood experiences are considered as well**.				
Students have increased access to academic supports **provided in a culturally and linguistically responsive manner**.				
The intervention team (tier 2 team) meets regularly to design and refine **CLR** tier 2 interventions in the building **using a CLR lens**.				
The intervention team (tier 2 team) provides training to families, school personnel, and students regarding interventions **that are culturally and linguistically responsive**.				
The intervention team (tier 2 team) members serve a coaching role to support implementation of **CLR** tier 2 practices among staff.				
Data (Tier 2 data practices are the same as tier 1.)	**0**	**1**	**2**	**3**
Data are regularly collected and analyzed **for signs of disproportionality in discipline, especially based on racial or ethnic demographics; intersectionality with special education status, sexual orientation, gender identification, sex, and socioeconomic status is also considered**.				
There is some type of schoolwide information system for collecting discipline and academic data about students **where the data can be disaggregated by different demographic subgroups, referring to personnel, time, setting, and behavior**.				
The Tiered Fidelity Inventory is used to assess how closely personnel apply the core features of PBIS **in combination with (or replaced by) this CLR-PBIS Fidelity Assessment Tool**.				

Source: Adapted from Center on PBIS, 2021d.

*Visit **go.SolutionTree.com/diversityandequity** for a free reproducible version of this figure.*

Assessment of Tier 3 Systems, Practices, and Data

Finally, it is essential to examine your school's tier 3 (intensive) systems, practices, and data for their alignment to CLR. To review, the focus on tier 3 is to provide intensive and individualized support to the very few students (up to approximately 5 percent) who may need it. Even with tiers 1 and 2 aligned to CLR, some students may still have behavioral needs that require a more tailored approach. It is important, though, that these tier 3 supports also align with CLR in order to be effective with underserved students. Furthermore, the process of referring students for tier 3 interventions must also be culturally and linguistically responsive to ensure that underserved groups are not inequitably referred or overrepresented. Racial disparities in students being referred to and receiving tier 3 supports indicate that you should change something about your school's PBIS systems, practices, and data.

Use the CLR-PBIS Fidelity Assessment Tool in figure 4.3 to assist you in assessing your school's tier 3 interventions for alignment with CLR. The plain font details the standard PBIS systems as described on the OSEP Technical Assistance Center on PBIS website (www.pbis.org), while the bold font delineates CLR alignment for each PBIS system, practice, or data source.

0—Not Implemented; 1—Partially Implemented; 2—Mostly Implemented; 3—Fully Implemented				
Systems	**0**	**1**	**2**	**3**
There is a multidisciplinary team (tier 3 team) with basic knowledge of problem solving **whose members are trained in CLR and CLR-SEL and have an understanding of healing-centered engagement (CLR trauma-sensitive practices).**				
The school's tier 3 team has a member with behavioral support expertise **that includes CLR, CLR-SEL, and an understanding of healing-centered engagement (CLR trauma-sensitive practices).**				
The tier 3 team monitors formal **CLR-PBIS** fidelity and outcome data collection, and **analyzes the data for signs of disproportionality.**				
The tier 3 team has a process for identifying individual personnel who require more intensive support in CLR (for example, teachers who are identified as persistently referring students to the office in a racially disproportionate way).				
Practices	**0**	**1**	**2**	**3**
Functional behavioral assessments **are implemented in a culturally and linguistically responsive manner.**				
Wraparound supports **are aligned to CLR.**				
Every practice has cultural and contextual fit **(is CLR aligned).**				
The school's tier 3 team meets regularly to ensure that (1) students who need additional support have access to those systems **and those systems are CLR**; and (2) students who receive tier 3 supports are successful.				
The school's tier 3 leadership team is led by someone with applied behavioral expertise, administrative authority, multiagency support experience, knowledge of students, knowledge about how the school operates across grade levels and programs, **and knowledge about CLR.**				

FIGURE 4.3: CLR-PBIS Fidelity Assessment Tool—tier 3 (intensive supports).

continued →

Practices	O	1	2	3
There is a problem-solving team (tier 3 student support team) for each student receiving tier 3 supports **that is trained in CLR**.				
The tier 3 student support team meets regularly to design and refine strategies specific to one student **and ensure that strategies are culturally and linguistically responsive**.				
Data (Tier 3 data practices are the same as tiers 1 and 2.)	O	1	2	3
Data are regularly collected and analyzed **for signs of disproportionality in discipline, especially based on racial or ethnic demographics; intersectionality with special education status, sexual orientation, gender identification, sex, and socioeconomic status is also considered**.				
There is some type of schoolwide information system for collecting discipline and academic data about students **where the data can be disaggregated by different demographic subgroups, referring to personnel, time, setting, and behavior**.				
The Tiered Fidelity Inventory is used to assess how closely personnel apply the core features of PBIS **in combination with (or replaced by) this CLR-PBIS Fidelity Assessment Tool**.				

Source: Adapted from Center on PBIS, 2021e.

*Visit **go.SolutionTree.com/diversityandequity** for a free reproducible version of this figure.*

Although the Center on PBIS (2021e) acknowledges the need for PBIS alignment with CLR, it is evident that more clarity on how to assess PBIS for CLR congruence is necessary. This section was meant to add that needed clarity for what to do next.

Activation

The third step is activation or, put another way, how to get the process of alignment started. The reality is that most schools will already have their PBIS system in place and will likely be entrenched in it. For some schools, aligning CLR to PBIS will feel like they are going back or starting over. Activation should send a clear message that substantial changes must occur, which may require, in most cases, a step or two back but for the purposes of moving forward. In other words, even though we call the final step *activation*, for most of you, it will be *re*activation. Activation means being resolved with the fact that you will have to take one, two, or even three steps back to move forward with alignment and assessment. The final step of activation should be revitalizing or mobilizing PBIS depending on your assessment results.

How do you activate after aligning and assessing? Activation is more a message than an action. It is a reflection to help determine your level or readiness. Activation is a final systems check but done in reflection. By going through the processes of aligning and assessing, you should very clearly know what you need to do in terms of next steps. The question, therefore, is not *how* anymore, but *Will* you? and *Can* you?

Following are three questions to consider for revitalizing or mobilizing your next version of PBIS. To align and assess successfully, you must answer *yes* to all three questions.

1. **Do you have the infrastructure (resources, leadership capacity, and flexibility) in place to make the necessary changes?** We have seen instances in which schools' grants have run out, so their funding source for PBIS implementation no longer exists. Without an adequate budget, renovating your PBIS will be a challenge. Another potential obstacle is the leadership's capacity to pull it off. Depending on the extent of the alignment, it may take a similar effort to the original PBIS implementation. You will need capable leaders to guide this process differently. For some, becoming CLR aligned is like turning around a ship, which means your system will have to be flexible, patient, and nimble. Plan on making changes in phases and what is within your capacity initially. You may not be able to do everything at once.

2. **Do you have the buy-in from all stakeholders?** Buy-in is almost always necessary for any innovation in education. This change is no different. Many stakeholders might respond negatively to PBIS revitalization because, to them, it might seem like just another attempted schoolwide change effort. The harsh reality, though, is that the biggest pushback will most likely come with your call to make PBIS culturally responsive. Some stakeholders are going to say, "If it ain't broke, don't fix it." But underneath that sentiment is a resistance to validating and affirming marginalized students. However you decide to roll out the revised plan, you must have buy-in from the classroom to the boardroom and beyond.

3. **Do you know your first step?** The first step you take will be the most important because it sets the tone for what is to come overall. The first step could range from convening a CLR-PBIS alignment task force or committee to conducting a professional development series in CLR, classroom management, or behavioral intervention. Be strategic and intentional about your first move. Be bold and brave. Think of the significance of first moves in other arenas, like playing a sport, giving a speech, or attending the first day of school. Your first action must send a message that CLR-aligned PBIS is here to stay.

Activation is really a way of saying *ready, set, go*. It is a systems check before starting the process after you have aligned and assessed.

Conclusion

Now you have your marching orders. Aligning your PBIS to CLR means implementing CLR authentically and using it as the zero tier or undergirding for your PBIS's three tiers. The good news is once you complete alignment and assessment, there are many opportunities for validation and affirmation within CLR-aligned PBIS, which we discuss in the next two chapters. Thus, the process of *how* continues in two concrete ways: (1) focusing on the opportunities for situational appropriateness, and (2) the language of situational appropriateness.

CHAPTER 5

Situationally Appropriate Opportunities Within PBIS

"A MATTER OF SITUATIONAL APPROPRIATENESS"
DANIEL RUSSELL JR.

While working as a teacher at CLAS, one of my students (let's call him D.J.) had to change schools mid-year. I was sad to see him go but understood why his family needed to change schools. Approximately one month later, I received a phone call from D.J.'s mother, who I had befriended as her son's teacher. She called to tell me something shocking that had occurred—D.J. had been sent to the office for the first time in his life.

This news shocked me because D.J. had always been a cooperative, engaged, and respectful student. His mother then explained why he had been sent to the office, and what she told me was appalling but not surprising. D.J. had been sent out because he responded to a teacher's question without raising his hand and waiting to be called on. As he had done so many times in my classroom, D.J. enthusiastically and spontaneously shouted out an answer to his teacher's question. Instead of validating and affirming his engagement and cultural behavior, however, the teacher publicly reprimanded him for "disrupting instruction" and "being disrespectful." The teacher then filled out an office disciplinary referral and sent D.J. to the office.

I told D.J.'s mother that I was dismayed but not surprised. I understood that D.J.'s new teacher was acting from her cultural frame of reference

> *and may have lacked the knowledge that D.J.'s behavior was not meant to be disrespectful. Furthermore, she missed an opportunity to validate and affirm D.J. while building and bridging him to the behavior that may have been situationally appropriate in the moment.*

Opportunities are conditions in which the probability of success is favorable. Therefore, situationally appropriate opportunities within PBIS refers to educators creating the conditions for students—particularly those from underserved backgrounds whose cultures differ from the dominant culture norms schools often reflect—to have an increased likelihood of behavioral success. Educators can do this by ensuring that underserved students' cultural behaviors are validated and affirmed through the way they are relate to, talk to, and teach students. Additionally, this involves educators building off underserved students' cultural assets by creating opportunities for using cultural behaviors in situationally appropriate ways within the school setting while also planning learning experiences to bridge underserved students to be situationally appropriate in terms of traditional school cultural norms.

As previously noted, in PBIS's three-tiered framework, tiers 2 and 3 must be layered on a solid tier 1 foundation. In fact, students should only be referred for tier 2 and 3 supports if tier 1 supports have not been effective. For underserved students who are disproportionately the recipients of office disciplinary referrals and other forms of exclusionary discipline, this means that all tier 1 practices must be culturally and linguistically responsive to be considered effective. Thus, educators must create situationally appropriate opportunities within PBIS to ensure that all tier 1 practices are fully culturally and linguistically responsive.

In this chapter, you will learn how to align the four essential tier 1 practices within CLR principles. Specifically, we will more deeply explore situational appropriateness, a concept critical to being culturally and linguistically responsive, with an emphasis on creating situationally appropriate opportunities within the PBIS framework. We will provide concrete examples of how you can ensure these PBIS practices are aligned with CLR, via what we call the *VABB framework*, so your school's unique PBIS framework has cultural and contextual fit.

How to Align Essential Tier 1 Practices With CLR

As previously discussed, we conceptualize CLR as the pre-tier, or zero tier, and base all aspects of PBIS on it, including tiers 1, 2, and 3. It is critical that schools undergird their PBIS frameworks with CLR not only to mitigate racial disproportionality in exclusionary discipline but also, more important, to transform school environments so they are truly validating, affirming, and welcoming for students from historically underserved cultural backgrounds (Gorski, n.d.).

If your school's PBIS is to effectively help your school achieve its chosen outcomes, you must implement key tier 1 practices with fidelity. These outcomes can range from a reduction in office disciplinary referrals to increased academic performance to decreased instances of bullying, depending on what your school's PBIS leadership team deems important (Center on PBIS, 2021b). The following four essential practices are core to tier 1 supports in PBIS and must be solidly in place before school personnel begin implementing tier 2 and 3 practices (Center on PBIS, 2021c). Not having critical practices in place is like building a house on a weak foundation.

1. Identify and select schoolwide behavioral expectations.
2. Explicitly teach students schoolwide behavioral expectations.
3. Implement procedures for encouraging cooperation with schoolwide behavioral expectations.
4. Define "problem" behaviors, and utilize procedures for discouraging them.

Identify and Select Schoolwide Behavioral Expectations

Most PBIS training and professional development emphasize the need for a school's PBIS leadership team to identify and establish a set of schoolwide behavioral expectations. In fact, according to the Center on PBIS (2021c), creating these shared understandings about desired behaviors is one of the PBIS leadership team's first tasks and must be in place before any subsequent tier 1 practices.

"ONE WORD SAYS IT ALL"
DANIEL RUSSELL JR.

In 2016, I took a vacation with my family to the Hawaiian island of Maui. This also happened to be the summer before my first academic year as dean (and I was to begin implementing PBIS at my school). My family and I were walking along a sidewalk in the town of Lahaina when we passed a school called the King Kamehameha III Elementary School. On the fence of the school was a sign that read Kūpono *in large letters, and underneath it were the words* integrity, honest, *and* fair. *I told my wife that it resembled what I had been learning about the PBIS tier 1 practice of setting schoolwide behavioral expectations. Moreover, I conjectured that it was a culturally responsive example of shared expectations. I took some photos to remind myself of what I saw, and then I later looked up what I could find about the school and the Hawaiian word Kūpono.*

Although the King Kamehameha III Elementary School did not use PBIS specifically, it did use the multitiered systems of supports (MTSS) framework. The values I saw on the sign were akin to schoolwide behavioral expectations that are a part of PBIS. I also learned that Kūpono is a Hawaiian word that means to be forthright, honest, and fair in your relationships with others (Hawaiian Convention Center Blog, 2012). For me, this coincided with what I had been learning about how PBIS needs to be culturally responsive and how to make it so. Specifically, it reinforced what I was learning about the need for schoolwide behavioral expectations to be culturally congruent with underserved students.

Unfortunately, often the chosen schoolwide behaviors in a school do not reflect the cultures of underserved students. Instead, they tend to reflect the values of the dominant (or White middle-class) group (Allen & Steed, 2016). For example, *be safe, be respectful, and be responsible* are three behavioral expectations widely found in schools utilizing PBIS. Many schools adopt them—maybe because they are used as examples on Center on PBIS's website (www.pbis.org) and in PBIS trainings, they align with the adopters' cultural paradigms, or the district leadership mandates them. Whatever the reasons for how schools choose schoolwide behavioral expectations, if schools are to implement PBIS in a truly culturally and linguistically responsive manner, then identifying and selecting shared behavioral expectations must have cultural and contextual fit within the local community. In other words, schools should not use a cookie-cutter approach, wherein every school must have the same schoolwide behavioral expectations that are not culturally congruent.

Culturally Congruent Schoolwide Principles

To create a sturdy CLR foundation for tier 1 practices, as well as validate and affirm the cultures of underserved students, schools must have schoolwide principles that are culturally congruent with their underserved students' cultures and not just with the dominant culture. Behavioral norms are culturally bound, and therefore, cannot be separated from culture in their selection (Banks & Obiakor, 2015). What this means is that because what educators consider to be acceptable or unacceptable behavior is culturally determined, we must take into consideration differing cultural perspectives when choosing a set of behavioral norms or expectations shared by all students. Schools that adopt a set of expected behaviors that are not culturally congruent with their underserved student populations' cultural beliefs and values, and only aligned to the cultural values of the dominant group, often experience cultural miscommunications between students and school staff, with underserved students being disproportionately affected (Betters-Bubon et al., 2016). Therefore, if the schoolwide behavioral expectations selected by a school's PBIS leadership team are incongruent with underserved students' cultural values, it can lead to misunderstandings that result in negative consequences, such as removing these students from the learning environment. For example, let's return to the behavioral expectation used in many schools that often leads to these cultural misunderstandings—*be respectful*. As previously noted, respect is a subjective value interpreted differently from varying cultural perspectives.

To help understand the cultural dynamics at play, consider the cultural behavior of realness and its relationship to the culturally interpreted value of respect. According to Hollie (2018), *realness* is defined as "how truth and authenticity are communicated to others" (p. 99). In some cultures, being direct is a form of realness and a way to show respect, while in other cultures, showing realness by being direct is considered disrespectful. Therefore, for instance, a teacher might perceive a student exhibiting realness by expressing his or her boredom with an unengaging lesson as disrespectful and reprimands him or her in some way. Yet, from the student's cultural perspective, he or she may have actually been showing respect by being real. So, if the teacher doesn't consider cultural subjectivity in interpreting respect, then he or she might reinforce respect in a way that aligns with the dominant culture. Moreover, the student that the teacher mistakenly perceived as being disrespectful often receives an unjust negative consequence, such as an office disciplinary referral.

The interpretation of subjective behavioral expectations, such as being respectful, can carry across the different cultural identities of teachers and other education staff as well. We are all influenced by cultural frames of reference and, therefore, interpret behaviors based on these frames. But we also may have adopted or learned to mirror the dominant culture determinations of various behavioral expectations. For instance, although an African American teacher may have been raised to view realness as a sign of respect, he or she may have adopted the dominant culture view that realness is disrespectful. The critical point is understanding that behavioral expectations are not culturally neutral, and it is essential that schools consider cultural differences in interpreting behavioral expectations when selecting its common, schoolwide PBIS behavioral expectations.

Diverse, Authentic, and Inclusive Student, Parent, and Community Involvement on PBIS Leadership Teams

When it comes to identifying and selecting a set of schoolwide behavioral expectations, the first question to consider is, Who is doing the identifying and selecting? Typically, a school forms a PBIS team of various stakeholders to lead PBIS implementation. This team consists of a coordinator, a school administrator, and teachers. It also should have diverse family and student representation, but this is often not the case. Either PBIS leadership teams do not include these essential stakeholders, or they do not typically include or authentically represent underserved students and their communities. In fact, their inclusion is nonexistent or nominal at best, meaning that even when they are included, the perspectives of parents and community members from underserved groups are often marginalized.

Bradley Quarles and Alisha Butler (2018) note that school administrators and personnel are often more responsive to parents with higher social status, such as affluent parents, and far less responsive to parents with less social cachet, such as families from lower socioeconomic levels. Therefore, if a school's PBIS is to be culturally and linguistically responsive, it is critical that it includes parents and community members of underrepresented groups in the process of selecting the school's shared behavioral expectations and developing the PBIS framework (Bal, 2018; Banks & Obiakor, 2015; Betters-Bubon et al., 2016; Eber et al., 2010; McIntosh, Moniz, Craft, Golby, & Steinwand-Deschambeault, 2014). If you are interested in learning an effective method for forming a balanced school-site PBIS leadership team that can select schoolwide behavioral expectations and build a CLR-PBIS framework, consider investigating the Learning Lab model developed by Aydin Bal of the University of Wisconsin–Madison (Bal, 2018; Bal, Afacan, & Cakir, 2018; Bal et al., 2012).

Several studies have shown that when underserved students, parents, and community members are authentically involved in selecting their school's culturally responsive behavioral expectations, not only do student behaviors improve and exclusionary discipline incidents lessen, but school environments also become more culturally validating and affirming. For instance, an article in *Canadian Journal of School Psychology* (McIntosh et al., 2014) details that when Chief Jimmy Bruneau School—a Canadian high school that predominantly serves Indigenous students—included local Indigenous Canadians in the selection of schoolwide expectations, thus ensuring cultural congruence, student behaviors showed improvement. This is because the school eliminated the previous cultural mismatch between students' cultural values and the school's. The resulting schoolwide behavioral expectations were called The Golden Rules and consisted of five culturally congruent values:

1. Have positive goals.
2. Respect yourself.
3. Respect others.

4. Respect your school and the environment.

5. Ask for help when you need it.

Another example of a school where parents and community members were consulted to ensure cultural alignment of the school's PBIS behavioral expectations was at a Jewish community day school. Researchers Kara E. McGoey, Avi Baron Munro, Allison McCobin, and Alison Miller (2016) describe the school's adoption of the Mensch Program, which was based on Jewish values. *Mensch* is a Yiddish word for "a person of good character" (McGoey et al., 2016, p. 137), and one of the school's behavioral expectations was to help its Jewish students become *menschen*, which means of good character. The researchers recount how overall behaviors in a Jewish day school significantly improved when the school adopted culturally responsive PBIS based on Jewish values (McGoey et al., 2016).

A final example where cultural alignment of schoolwide behavioral expectations occurred was at our CLR laboratory school, CLAS. We adopted the African-centered principles of Ma'at, which we referred to as the *righteous principles* (see chapter 1, pages 26–27). Because these principles, or behavioral expectations, culturally validated and affirmed our Black students, this minimized cultural misunderstandings, thus resulting in better student behavioral outcomes. At CLAS, the selection of the shared schoolwide behavioral expectations was not done in collaboration with parents, though, as has been described in the previous examples. This is because they were selected in advance by our founders, who themselves were members of the African American community and had children who would be attending CLAS, and were specifically chosen to be culturally congruent. Although other parents were not involved in the selection of the school's behavioral expectations, they chose to enroll their children in CLAS with the advanced knowledge about our righteous principles and agreement with them.

So, what's the main takeaway? If you want your school's PBIS framework to be truly culturally and linguistically responsive, then you must authentically involve students, parents, and community members from underserved groups in identifying and selecting culturally congruent schoolwide behavioral expectations. No doubt it will be a challenging process, especially if such authentic inclusion and power sharing are not typical for your school, but focus and perseverance toward the goal of creating equitable results for *all* students should serve as motivation.

Also, if your school already has a set of schoolwide expectations, you may be wondering if it is too late to do something about it. It is never too late. In fact, a PBIS framework is not supposed to be set in stone. It is a living framework that educators should constantly revisit to ensure it is responsive to the school's population, especially when student demographics shift. Sugai and colleagues (2012) emphasize that a school's PBIS framework must adapt to the "culture and context" of the school (p. 202). We can also describe this as PBIS having cultural and contextual fit. So, that means whether your school is just starting out developing a PBIS framework or it already has one in place, this framework must reflect the cultures of your students and the context of your school's community.

Explicitly Teach Students Schoolwide Behavioral Expectations

After your school's PBIS leadership team (which we hope at this point you are beginning to conceptualize as your CLR-PBIS leadership team) has identified and selected culturally congruent schoolwide behavioral expectations, the next major task is to explicitly teach these expectations to students (Center on PBIS, 2021c). Teachers must ground teaching of these behavioral expectations in the VABB framework and the concept of situational appropriateness. Otherwise, students may not truly learn these expectations. Or worse, students may conceptualize the behavioral expectations as merely right or wrong.

Rather than developing simplistic binary thinking about behavior, students require a more nuanced understanding of whether a behavior is situationally appropriate for a particular context. You need to build this level of metacognitive awareness about behavior in your lessons through explicit instruction of schoolwide behavioral expectations while utilizing CLR instructional methods. Using this approach, teachers should encourage students to actively think about what behavior is most appropriate for any particular situation, whether they are at home or in school. Students should be asking themselves, "What is the most appropriate behavior for this situation?"

Besides teaching schoolwide behavior expectations as they apply to the classroom setting, schools often teach behavioral expectations for common areas such as the cafeteria, bathrooms, hallways, and more. This instruction typically occurs during the first couple of weeks of school, after holiday breaks, and whenever necessary as evidenced by students' behaviors. Classroom teachers, specials teachers, counselors, paraprofessionals, administrators, and other staff all may be in charge of leading these lessons. Regardless of who teaches the behavioral expectations for each common area of the school, these individuals must understand why they need to ground these lessons in the VABB framework and the concept of situational appropriateness. They must also know *how* to do so, which involves the following CLR elements listed:

- Educators must ground all lessons about schoolwide behavioral expectations in the linked concepts of situational appropriateness and cultureswitching.

- Educators must use modeling and storytelling to teach schoolwide behavioral expectations.

- Educators must use instructional strategies aligned with CLR in all lessons to optimize learning.

- Educators should use a three-step process for communicating behavioral expectations: (1) teach expected behaviors for each situation, (2) provide students with opportunities to practice these behaviors, and (3) provide feedback to reinforce these behaviors (Sprick, 2009).

Contextualize Lessons on Behavioral Expectations in Situational Appropriateness and Cultureswitching

To begin, any lessons about schoolwide behavioral expectations must first be contextualized in terms of situational appropriateness and cultureswitching to be most effective. Let's first revisit the definition of *situational appropriateness*, which is "the concept of determining which cultural or linguistic behaviors are most appropriate for a situation *without giving up one's culture and language*" (Hollie, 2018, p. 52). Now, let's dive deeper into this definition. Notice how the qualifier *most* is used before *appropriate*? This word is significant because it highlights that different behaviors could be appropriate for any given context, but one may be considered the most appropriate of them all. Note, too, that *appropriate* is not the same as *right* or *wrong* or *incorrect* or *correct*. Instead, its synonyms are *suitable*, *befitting*, *timely*, and *authentic*. How do you tell, then, what is the most appropriate behavior for a specific context?

The key is understanding the cultural dynamics of the context. What teachers, students, and others consider to be most suitable behavior is typically determined by cultural dynamics, so it is important to ascertain what cultural elements are valued in any given circumstance. Sometimes, the most appropriate behavior is one aligned with the cultural behaviors of underserved students. More often than not, in the school setting, what is considered most appropriate is aligned with dominant (or White middle class) cultural values. For example, in an elementary setting, students are often expected to walk through the hallway in straight lines, with hands at their sides, and without talking, because these are considered the most appropriate behaviors for the hallway setting. In fact, in many schools we have visited that use PBIS, posters with these behavioral expectations for the hallway are displayed throughout the school and an internet search turns up many examples from different schools.

Yet, a key issue with hallway behavioral expectations such as this is that they do not consider varying contexts in which cultural behaviors of underserved students could be situationally appropriate as well. Schools often consider walking in silent and straight lines the most or only appropriate behavior for elementary school hallways because that aligns with traditional school norms, but walking and talking without lines could be the most appropriate hallway behavior in a specific situation (for example, it is the end of the school day, and there is no one to interrupt) when the cultural behavior of sociocentrism is valued (students need to connect with their peers). Hence, it is essential to contextualize any teaching of schoolwide behavioral expectations within the concept of situational appropriateness to prevent the perpetuation of dominant culture norms. (We will elaborate on this example scenario in chapter 6, page 109.)

No discussion of situational appropriateness is complete without also addressing the related concept of cultureswitching. We define *cultureswitching* as "switching from one cultural or linguistic behavior to another for the purpose of being situationally appropriate"

(Hollie, 2018, pp. 52–53). When considering these two linked concepts, you can think of situational appropriateness as a noun, or state of being, and cultureswitching as a verb, or the act of changing to be situationally appropriate. However, note that cultureswitching as a verb should not be confused with codeswitching and its historical deficit connotation. Recall that we previously explained that the commonly used term *codeswitching* is a deficit term that implies something is wrong, bad, or less with the home culture or language (Hollie, 2018). In sum, situational appropriateness and cultureswitching cannot occur without validation and affirmation of the home culture or language.

Now, let's apply the concept of cultureswitching to the previous hallway scenario. Teachers may inform students that the most appropriate behavior for when they are in the hallway, on the way to the library, while other classes are in session is to move in quiet and straight lines. Then, teachers or other staff could ask students to cultureswitch to cooperate (and not just comply) with these expectations. Conversely, when the context changes, teachers and staff could tell students that it is a time of day when no classes might be disturbed by talking in the hallway and to cultureswitch so they can talk with their peers. They might not even expect straight lines at this time. Again, the context (time, place, and circumstances) of the situation determines what behaviors are appropriate and how students may cultureswitch to be situationally appropriate.

What does applying situational appropriateness and cultureswitching with the CLR-PBIS and VABB frameworks look like? Again, it is considered standard PBIS tier 1 practice to explicitly teach students schoolwide behavioral expectations (or what we call *ways of being*) and how they look in different situations in the classroom and common areas (or what we call *ways of doing*). A sample lesson for the hallway example might look like the following.

1. Ask students to recall the schoolwide behavioral expectations.
2. Have students share what these expectations might look like in the hallway.
3. Have students consider and share if these expectations could be different depending on the situation.
4. Emphasize that the situation determines the most appropriate behaviors for the hallway.
5. Have students practice cultureswitching for different hallway scenarios, and provide positive, reinforcing feedback.

This lesson illustrates how situational appropriateness and cultureswitching apply to a minilesson about how to exhibit expected behaviors in a common area. Also, this particular example may be more applicable to the elementary setting, and therefore, may need to be adapted for middle school and high school settings. Besides considering a contextual factor, such as the setting, this lesson is not fully culturally and linguistically responsive because it does not include the use of CLR instructional activities . . . *yet*.

It is important that you incorporate instructional activities that are CLR in expected behavior lessons, as with any lesson on academic content that you teach. Teachers cannot expect lessons that rely just on traditional instructional strategies to effectively help underserved students learn behavioral expectations. Figure 5.1 shows a sample CLR-infused minilesson on behavioral expectations; it illustrates how to infuse CLR activities into the previous minilesson.

Lesson Steps	CLR Instructional Activities	VABB Cultural or School Behaviors
1. Ask students to list the schoolwide behavioral expectations.	a. Moment of silence b. Shout Out	a. Individual success b. Orality and verbal expressiveness
2. Have students share what these expectations might look like in the hallway.	a. Musical Shares b. Pick-a-Stick	a. Kinesthetics, sociocentrism b. Spontaneity, dynamic attention span
3. Have students consider and share if these expectations could be different depending on the situation.	a. Put Your Two Cents In b. Raise a hand	a. Subjectivity, dynamic attention span, turn taking b. Prompted, individual success
4. Emphasize that the situation determines the most appropriate behaviors for the hallway.	a. Direct instruction	a. Prompted, stationary
5. Have students practice cultureswitching for different hallway scenarios, and provide positive, reinforcing feedback.	a. Role play	a. Kinesthetics, collaboration, communalism

FIGURE 5.1: Sample CLR-infused minilesson on behavioral expectations.
*Visit **go.SolutionTree.com/diversityandequity** for a free reproducible version of this figure.*

Of course, this minilesson just provides broad strokes for a potential CLR-infused lesson that teaches students the behavioral expectations for one particular context, but the lesson utilizes the concepts of situational appropriateness and the VABB framework. As you do this with your students, you need to think in advance of all the classroom and common-area contexts for which you need to teach minilessons about behavioral expectations.

This is a core PBIS tier 1 practice required to establish a solid foundation for your school's CLR-PBIS framework. Without it, your tiers 2 and 3 supports will be highly weakened and overwhelmed. Also, as modeled in the example, rather than simply tell students the expected behaviors for different situations, engage students in collaboratively creating these descriptions of situationally appropriate behavior; this is truly culturally and linguistically responsive. This takes time to do well, but the time invested at the beginning of the school year (and at other critical points, such as after holiday breaks, field trips, and testing windows) will pay substantial dividends manifested as improved classroom climate, more student engagement, more time when students are learning, and less time when you are responding to significant behavioral issues.

Don't Just Tell It, Teach It

Besides infusing lessons that teach behavioral expectations with CLR instructional activities, teachers also need to teach these lessons strategically, just as they teach lessons on academic content. Karen Robbie and Erik Maki (Northeast PBIS Network, 2020) recommend considering the following questions when teaching schoolwide behavioral expectations (the behavior matrix). For those who recall from your fundamental understanding of PBIS, the behavior matrix is a detailed description of the behaviors expected in various settings in the common areas of the school and contexts within the classroom. These specific expectations are aligned with the schoolwide behavioral expectations—such as *be safe, be respectful, be responsible*—and usually are displayed in some kind of chart. An internet search results in a wide variety of behavioral matrices developed by different schools.

1. When will you teach the behaviors?
2. Where will you teach the behaviors?
3. Who will teach the behaviors?
4. How will you teach the behaviors?
5. How will you measure student learning of the behaviors?

We have now discussed *how* and *why* to infuse expected behavior lessons with CLR using the VABB framework. Next, consider *who* might best teach these lessons so they are effective with culturally and linguistically diverse students.

This chapter focuses on question 4: *How will you teach the behaviors?* Lessons designed to teach behavioral expectations are most effective if they follow a three-step process, like this one drawn from Sprick's (2009) CHAMPS model:

1. Teach and model the behavior expectations.
2. Provide time for students to practice the expected behaviors while you monitor them.
3. Provide effective feedback to reinforce the behaviors.

Teach and Model the Behavior Expectations

As noted in chapter 2 (page 37), modeling behaviors is a CLR-aligned method for reinforcing expected behaviors (Kozleski, 2010). Additionally, Kozleski (2010) explains that the use of storytelling to teach and reinforce desired behaviors is a culturally congruent practice; therefore, teachers should use stories (for example, cultural parables, culturally authentic texts, culturally authentic television show episodes or movies, or personal narratives) to help teach their schoolwide behavioral expectations. Say, for example, your diverse, authentic, and inclusive CLR-PBIS leadership team has chosen perseverance as a culturally congruent schoolwide behavior. You might use an African proverb such as, "Knowledge is like a lion; it cannot be easily embraced," to frame a lesson on the meaning of perseverance and how it applies to working hard on assignments.

Provide Time for Students to Practice the Expected Behaviors While You Monitor Them

All too often, teachers do not provide students opportunities to practice behaviors they want them to learn, and they wonder why the students do not exhibit them. Like with any other skill (for example, writing a paragraph, shooting a free throw, or solving a multistep mathematics problem), students need opportunities to practice the behaviors you expect them to exhibit. While students are practicing, you should allow them to try and fail.

Drawing from Carol Dweck's (2016) seminal work on growth mindset, it is critical for students' optimal learning that you view mistakes students make while practicing in a positive light. While students are practicing situationally appropriate behaviors, you must actively monitor students by circulating and observing. By doing this, you can gather data about your students to use in helping them master desired behaviors. *Note that monitoring is not surveillance.* You are not looking to catch students doing something "wrong." Rather, aligning with a positive and proactive CLR approach, you are intentionally looking for how students are cooperating with the most appropriate behaviors for each individual situation so you can affirm and acknowledge students' cooperation in order to reinforce shared behavioral expectations.

Provide Effective Feedback to Reinforce the Behaviors

You cannot skip the last step of this process if students are to truly learn from the instructional sequence. You must provide students with feedback, based on your observations, during the practicing and monitoring step. Unfortunately, this is an often-neglected step in helping students learn expected behaviors at school. Interestingly, in other contexts, teachers often provide the necessary feedback. For example, if a student misses a critical step while doing a mathematics computation, you might demonstrate which step he or she missed. In another context, a football player might be throwing a ball using the wrong grip, so you provide feedback on how to properly grip the ball. The same principle applies to students learning the behaviors you teach; they need specific feedback.

Randy Sprick (2009) notes that teachers should give corrective feedback calmly, immediately, and consistently for students to master a desired behavior. He also explains that they should deliver this feedback in a positive, accurate, and specific manner and make the feedback contingent on the student's performance of the desired behavior. Finally, he emphasizes that feedback should be both collective (acknowledging the class or group as a whole) and summative (given at the end of each lesson and coupled with goal setting regarding the behavior). Providing collective feedback is especially important for students who come from cultures that value communalism, wherein group success is more important than individual success (Hollie, 2018). According to Andrew Moemeka (1998), "American Indians, Australian Aborigines, Canadian Indians, Eskimos, Southeast Asians, and those in the Caribbean countries" (p. 125) are examples of various cultural groups that value communalism. If you want students to master situationally appropriate behavior, then it is critical you give them specific, reinforcing feedback and not just assume they learned what you taught.

Implement Procedures for Encouraging Cooperation With Schoolwide Behavioral Expectations

According to the Center on PBIS (2021c), after your school has established its shared behavioral expectations, it is time to create "procedures for encouraging expected behaviors" as part of your tier 1 practices. In other words, you need to decide how you will acknowledge students when they exhibit the expected behaviors. Affirming students when they demonstrate the desired behaviors is crucial to increasing the frequency of such behaviors and creating safe and positive school cultures and climates (Missouri School-wide Positive Behavior Support, 2018; Sprick, 2009). But how do schools do this in a culturally and linguistically responsive manner?

The Center on PBIS (2021c) recommends schools adopt a token system to encourage compliance with schoolwide behavioral expectations. From a CLR perspective, this is problematic. In chapter 2 (page 37), we argued that the traditional PBIS framework is not inherently culturally and linguistically responsive because it is banked on extrinsic rewards and it focuses on compliance rather than cooperation. We noted the recommendation to use a token system as a type of "gotcha" approach, wherein teachers reward students when they catch them displaying desired behaviors. This may conflict with culturally and linguistically responsive practices in which teachers validate and affirm students for cooperating with norms rather than reward them extrinsically. Moreover, this strategy lessens in effectiveness as students get older and progress developmentally. We have heard from numerous educators with whom we work that many of their students from the upper elementary grades to middle school and beyond are not as motivated by the use of tokens and will even refuse accepting them.

Next, recall that when it comes to being culturally and linguistically responsive, cooperation, and not compliance, is the name of the game. In a CLR approach, teachers inspire students to cooperate with culturally congruent behavioral expectations; they do not force them to comply with a set of rules. Teachers encourage students to choose to behave in the most situationally appropriate way because of intrinsic reasons rather than external factors. Fay and Funk (1995) address this in their love and logic approach to classroom management. They argue that internal controls and values are more powerful than external reinforcement.

How do you then *encourage* students to choose to cooperate with schoolwide expected behaviors that are culturally congruent rather than merely comply with them? First, you need to go back to how you began developing a CLR-PBIS framework for your school—by getting authentic involvement from a representative and inclusive stakeholder group that includes students, parents, and community members. Just as this diverse CLR-PBIS leadership team selects culturally resonant behavioral expectations for the whole school, it should also identify and select culturally aligned ways for promoting and acknowledging these behaviors.

Kent McIntosh and colleagues (2014) describe that when school officials at Chief Jimmy Bruneau School—a Canadian high school that predominantly serves Indigenous students—worked with tribal elders to culturally align their PBIS framework with the values and practices of the Indigenous community, they included a positive recognition system. In this example, the school used a type of token system, but it was in full alignment with the Indigenous community's values and practices. Moreover, it provided students with contingent positive attention (specific praise) for cooperating with culturally congruent norms and not merely complying with rules that just reflected dominant culture norms.

Similarly, at CLAS, we publicly affirmed students for exhibiting our culturally grounded schoolwide values—the righteous principles—in classrooms, in common areas, and during a regular recognition ceremony we called the Righteous Are Rewarded. In this ceremony, we acknowledged every student for cooperating with our shared schoolwide values in one way or another. These recognition ceremonies or assemblies need to be inclusive of *all* students and recognize them for exhibiting cultural behaviors as well as traditional school cultural behaviors. Again, according to many teachers we have worked with in schools using PBIS, underserved students, especially those with the greatest needs, are often left out of celebrations and go unrecognized, which further contributes to their use of resistance and avoidance as coping mechanisms.

Giving students specific praise is another standard PBIS tier 1 practice for encouraging expected behaviors recommended by the Center on PBIS (2021c). Kohn (2018) emphasizes, however, that praise can be problematic if used as a means for external control and eliciting student compliance. Instead, he asserts that praise, or positive feedback, should be used in a way that provides students with the "straightforward information" (p. 96) they need for knowing how well they have done a task, or in this case, how well they have followed behavior expectations for a specific context. This approach to encouraging expected behavior with positive informational feedback is considered to be culturally and linguistically responsive to underserved students.

In a CLR approach, then, students must receive feedback to know when they are exhibiting situationally appropriate behavior. As Kohn (2018) cautions, this feedback cannot be generic, such as "good job" or "nice." Rather, students need to receive information in the form of feedback that explicitly lets them know what they did and how they did in relation to the behavioral expectations for the specific situation. In other words, the feedback needs to be contextual. For example, instead of saying something non-specific such as, "Good job, Imani," a teacher might tell a student, "Imani, I noticed you were practicing our schoolwide expectation of justice by standing up for your classmate when she was being teased." This level of specificity helps students more concretely connect the feedback to their actions. Moreover, it shifts the attention away from students focusing on getting the teacher's approval to connecting the feedback to the behavior itself. Here are a few more examples of specific and positive feedback aligned with CLR:

- "Juan, I see that you are taking time to show your work on your mathematics assignment."

- "Today, class, you were all showing responsibility by submitting your assignments on time."

- "Jasmin, tonight when you get home, tell your parents that you were caring for your classmate today by helping her carry her books."

- "Amirah, Jacob, and Rosa, thank you for showing respect for our environment by picking up the trash you saw on the playground . . . and without anyone asking you to do it."

- "Hey Malik, you really worked hard on your essay, and I can tell how you are practicing our schoolwide behavior of always trying your best."

As an element of your school's tier 1 practices for encouraging expected behavior through specific positive feedback, the ratio of positive interactions to corrections of "problem" behaviors is important to keep in mind. Different ratios have been suggested—such as 3:1 by Sprick (2009), 4:1 by the Missouri School-wide Positive Behavior Support (2018), and 5:1 by Stephen Ray Flora (2000)—but regardless of the ratio, it's most critical to remember that students need to receive more positive feedback than corrective (negative) feedback (Sabey, Charlton, & Charlton, 2019). According to Sprick (2009), one reason for offering more positive feedback is that students may need attention. Attention could be in the form of contextual feedback, or it could be noncontingent feedback (not related to any specific behavior). The key is that students feel acknowledged and not invisible or neglected.

Another reason to offer more positive feedback is that it counteracts the brain's neg-ativity bias. In *Culturally Responsive Teaching and the Brain*, Zaretta Hammond (2015) notes that the brain "remembers and responds to negative experiences up to three times more than positive experiences" (p. 113). Therefore, to offset this natural tendency toward the negative, students must receive positive feedback, or specific praise, several times more than they receive corrective or negative feedback. Finally, using more positive feedback is particularly crucial for culturally and linguistically diverse students, who all too often experience negative messages, both explicit and implicit, about who they are. By having more positive interactions with teachers and staff, students feel more validated and affirmed, which is a core aspect of CLR.

Following are some final reminders about providing specific feedback for positively reinforcing schoolwide behavioral expectations in a culturally and linguistically respon-sive manner.

- First and foremost, underserved students should receive equitable feedback for cooperating with both culturally congruent behavioral expectations and the dominant culture norms, which are typically encoded in traditional school behavioral expectations. This is where the VABB framework becomes useful. Students need to be validated and affirmed when they exhibit culturally aligned behavioral expectations and built and bridged to schoolwide behavioral expectations that are not culturally aligned.

- Specific positive feedback should not just be for individual students. Because many underserved groups come from collectivist cultures in which communalism is a deep cultural value, students should also receive positive feedback for group (for example, team, class, or grade level) cooperation with schoolwide expectations.

- It is important that the majority of adults interacting with students provide specific positive feedback. The Center on PBIS (2021c) recommends that 90 percent or more of faculty and staff positively acknowledge students when they observe them exhibiting desired behaviors. The ubiquitous feedback increases the probability of students valuing cooperation within the shared norms of conduct.

- Educators should deliver specific positive feedback in a developmentally appropriate, unpatronizing, and authentic manner. While a gushing, higher-pitched acknowledgment of cooperation may be effective with kindergartners, middle schoolers, unsurprisingly, may react negatively to such an approach.

- Educators should give feedback in a way that does not come across as sarcastic or demeaning. Even feedback that is supposed to be encouraging can be interpreted as offensive talk or even a racial microaggression. For example, complimenting a high school student for taking out a sheet of paper ("Great job, Manuel, for getting out your paper on time. That's showing responsibility") can be interpreted as having low expectations, patronizing, or manipulating the student because it is for such menial behavior. For older students, Karen Sheriff LeVan and Marrisa King (2016) recommend engaging in discourse with students about how they prefer to receive feedback to increase the probability that the feedback is positively received.

Developmentally and individually, some students may feel embarrassed by receiving public feedback for cooperating with behavioral expectations. Sprick (2009) notes that this could be attributed to a need to preserve a "tough guy" identity or difficulties handling success. This could also be attributed to students' deep cultural norms that value group accolades more than individual recognition.

Now, that does not mean you should avoid giving specific positive feedback, but it does mean you should learn how to give it effectively in a culturally and linguistically responsive way. Ultimately, students will be more likely to respond well to feedback when you foster positive relationships with students, provide feedback in a manner authentic to your personality (meaning you are not trying to fake it), validate and affirm students when they cooperate with the culturally congruent schoolwide expectations, and equitably deliver positive acknowledgments (no privileging some students over others).

Does this mean you should never use extrinsic rewards to encourage expected behaviors as part of your school's CLR-PBIS tier 1 practices? The answer is, it depends. It depends on whether using extrinsic rewards is culturally congruent with the cultural practices and values of your students. Moreover, Kohn (2018) exhorts against the use of extrinsic rewards because of the lack of empirical research that supports their effectiveness and evidence suggesting their potential harm to student motivation, particularly when poorly applied.

That being said, the use of extrinsic rewards to encourage cooperation with schoolwide behavioral expectations or situationally appropriate cultural behaviors may be effective, but only under specific conditions. First, use extrinsic rewards strategically and not just generally. For example, a group of elementary students might be struggling with taking responsibility for cleaning up after themselves in the classroom. You could temporarily tie extrinsic rewards to the objective of changing this behavior. In the elementary setting, this may take the form of extra recess time when the students achieve and maintain mastery of the expected behavior. In the secondary setting, this would entail engaging students in a discussion of the expected behavior and collaborating on an extrinsic reward. Again, be cautious about mitigating perceptions of coercion and low expectations.

Once students consistently demonstrate the expected behavior, gradually remove the extrinsic reward. Sprick (2009) recommends that to be effective, you should gradually remove extrinsic rewards because rewards that persist for a long time lose their potency in encouraging desired behaviors. Think of them like prescriptions in your medicine cabinet that have been there for years and are far past their expiration date. They may still have an effect on your symptoms, but that effect will be greatly diminished.

Next, extrinsic rewards may be effective if you use them unpredictably. This is a practice called *positive intermittent rewards*, and the unexpected extrinsic compensation for cooperation with norms may increase the frequency of this cooperation (Orlowski, 2020; Sprick, 2009). According to the documentary *The Social Dilemma* (Orlowski, 2020) social media platforms, slot machines, and well-designed video games apply this principle to keep you engaged. When you receive an unexpected reward, you are more likely to check your social media posts or keep playing. So, in the school context, this could manifest as a teacher randomly telling her high school science class that they do not have homework for the evening because they worked so hard in class. Therefore, intermittently rewarding students may further motivate them to cooperate with shared expectations, but this comes with a caveat. As Kohn (2018) cautions, the effectiveness of the use of extrinsic rewards, regardless of how they are administered, has not been consistently empirically supported and could be misused to try and control students' behaviors rather supporting students in developing intrinsically motivated self-regulation of their behavior.

Finally, extrinsic rewards may be appropriate if they align with students' cultural values. When the extrinsic rewards you use match deep cultural beliefs, they are more culturally resonant, and thus, culturally and linguistically diverse students value them more.

Define "Problem" Behaviors and Utilize Procedures for Discouraging Them

The final essential practice of a solid tier 1 foundation for your CLR-PBIS framework to address is what the Center on PBIS (2021c) refers to as a "continuum of procedures for discouraging 'problem' behaviors." Let's turn our attention to what we mean by "problem" behavior. This understanding is necessary in order to answer important tier 1 questions such as, "What are classroom-managed (minor) problems versus office-managed (major) problems?" or "How do you handle 'problem' behaviors when they arise?" and answer them in a culturally and linguistically responsive manner. Also, in answering queries like these, we will once again be applying the concepts of situational appropriateness and cultureswitching and the VABB framework.

Define "Problem" Behaviors With a CLR Lens

What is the problem with *problem*? Defining a behavior as a problem can involve both implicit and explicit biases, since educators' perceptions of which behaviors are problematic (or *wrong* or *challenging* and labeled "problem" behaviors) stem from their cultural frames of reference. How educators are culturally socialized greatly impacts how they perceive behavior, so much so that they may not even be aware of how these societal influences, such as family, friends, media, stories, and teachers, shape how they distinguish which behaviors are good or appropriate and which are bad or problematic. This is especially salient in the context of school, where differences in cultural perceptions of behaviors come into contact and conflict and, all too often, students from underserved communities bear the negative impact (for example, overrepresentation in office discipline referrals, suspensions, expulsions, and involvement of law enforcement). Teachers' subjective judgments of underserved students', especially Black students', behaviors are a primary factor in racial disproportionality in exclusionary discipline (Anyon et al., 2014; Bal, 2016; Eber et al., 2010; Parsons, 2018). To better understand this, note the following example in which a teacher's subjective judgment regarding the cultural behavior of spontaneity influences how she handles the situation.

A teacher explains the causes of the U.S. Civil War when an African American student spontaneously shares a personal connection to the topic. In response, the teacher admonishes the student for being rude by "blurting out," rather than raising his hand and waiting to be called on to share. The student, feeling disrespected, especially in front of his peers, attempts to save face by saying, "This lesson is stupid anyway." The teacher angrily responds by telling the student to go to the office as she writes up an office discipline referral for the subjectively defined behaviors of defiance, disrespect, and disruptive behavior.

Although this example is based on the cultural behavior of spontaneity, note that the student was not referred to the office for exhibiting spontaneity. Rather, the "problem" behavior identified on the office disciplinary referral was for the subjectively defined behaviors of defiance, disrespect, and disruption. When looking at data for office disciplinary referrals (ODRs), such cultural behaviors are not identified, so we are left to infer the student's actual behavior. What we do know though, is that studies have shown that Black students are referred to the office far more often than White students for subjective behaviors (like disrespect) than objective behaviors (like leaving school without permission).

For example, Lucille Eber, Gita Upreti, and Jennifer Rose (2010) found that out of 6,172 ODRs at a middle school in Illinois for subjective reasons, Black students received 2,679 (43.4 percent) of the referrals as opposed to White students who received 1,684 (27.3 percent) of the referrals. Jamilia J. Blake, Bettie Ray Butler, Chance W. Lewis, and

Alicia Darensbourg (2011) identified a similar pattern when examining ODR data for a Midwestern urban school district. Black female students received 1,315 ODRs for the subjectively-defined behavior of disobedience and 532 ODRs for defiance, as opposed to White female students receiving 614 and 115 ODRs, respectively. This disparity is particularly significant, as Black female students comprised just 21 percent of the enrollment as opposed to White female students, who comprised 26 percent. Note that 90 percent of the teachers were White.

This scenario exemplifies the issue with defining behaviors as "problems." Such definitions require a deep understanding of how culture mediates people's perceptions of what a "problem" behavior is and knowledge of how the cultural behaviors of underserved students differ from those privileged in schools as "normal" or "traditional." In this situation, the student is exhibiting the cultural behaviors of spontaneity by shouting out and field dependence by connecting the lesson to his own experiences. Hollie (2019b) describes *field dependence* (that is, relevance) as "an orientation toward externally defined goals and reinforcements compared to the social and cultural relevance to one's own experiences" (p. 2).

The teacher, because of either implicit or explicit biases toward these cultural behaviors (cultural assets) stemming from a lack of knowledge about cultural behaviors, perceives them as problems and reacts punitively, leading to an escalating cycle that results in unjustly removing the student from the classroom. How could the teacher handle this situation in a culturally and linguistically responsive way? We will return to this scenario after we finish unpacking the definition of "problem" behaviors. But first, let's discuss the minor and major behaviors.

Identify Minor and Major Behaviors Within Situational Appropriateness

In their original PBIS conception, the terms *minor* and *major* are used as adjectives to describe the level of seriousness of a "problem" behavior. For example, uttering a curse word once is considered a minor behavior, whereas angrily punching another student in the face is considered a major behavior. All too often, though, teachers and staff transform these terms into *nouns*. For example, teachers may say that a student has two minors today, or that a student committed a major. In essence, when teachers use *minor* and *major* in this way, they liken students' behavioral missteps to strikes in baseball by saying, for example, "That's your second minor today" or "He got three majors today. He's out of this class."

When teachers do this, it causes them to lose focus on the nature of students' behaviors and the underlying motivations for or functions of them. Moreover, it causes teachers to perceive and respond to students' behaviors in a rigid rather than flexible, culturally and linguistically responsive manner. Using the terms *minor* and *major* as nouns causes teachers to be reactive and use decontextualized responses that do not effectively address the specific issue or behavior. Instead, when teachers use these terms appropriately as adjectives that describe a behavior's level of seriousness, it puts them in a frame of mind to respond with an intervention tailored to the specific behavior and not just a generic intervention.

The foundational tier 1 practice of clearly defining "problem" behaviors also involves distinguishing between minor behaviors managed by staff (for example, teachers and playground aides) and major behaviors managed by the office (for example, school administration). Again, educators must determine these categories in a culturally and linguistically responsive manner and in collaboration with a diverse CLR-PBIS leadership team to ensure they do not misidentify cultural behaviors as needing staff or office management.

For example, educators often identify minor noncompliance as a staff-managed "problem" behavior. *Minor noncompliance* is when a student does not follow a teacher directive such as *sit down* or *stop running in the classroom*. The problem, though, is that teachers (or other staff, such as playground supervisors) often subjectively determine what behaviors constitute minor noncompliance. Therefore, because noncompliance is so vague in its determination due to its subjective definition, it should not be listed as "problem" behavior to be either staff or office managed.

Consider the following scenario that exemplifies a student exhibiting the cultural behavior of directness, which the teacher misinterprets as noncompliance.

> *Sarai has been sitting awhile and needs movement, so she begins to rock in her seat. Her teacher asks, "Sarai, would you like to stop rocking in your seat?" Sarai replies, "No." The teacher, who is operating from his dominant cultural paradigm of indirectness, perceives this as noncompliance and issues a verbal reprimand (per his predetermined hierarchy of consequences for minor behaviors). Sarai, operating from her cultural paradigm of realness and directness, insists she did not do anything wrong and responds angrily (and justly so) to the verbal reprimand. The teacher then warns Sarai that she will be sent to the office if she continues to not comply with his directions.*

Schools must be clear about how they categorize behaviors (cultural or not cultural) when determining whether "problem" behaviors are staff managed (minor) or office managed (major). Lack of clarity can result in cultural misunderstandings. Furthermore, such cultural conflicts are a key variable in the overrepresentation of underserved students in office discipline referrals.

How can teachers and other school staff avoid such cultural misunderstandings? Recall the Three Columns activity in chapter 1 (page 33), which can help educators challenge their mindsets and identify their blindspots regarding cultural behaviors. We will now build on that activity by connecting it to a similar one recommended by Leverson and colleagues (2019) called the Pi chart (called a Pi chart because the chart resembles the Greek symbol *Pi*.) Leverson and colleagues' Pi chart includes the categories of *staff-managed "problem" behaviors*, *office-managed "problem" behaviors*, and *situationally inappropriate behaviors*. This is a step in the CLR direction that misses the mark because of how it handles situationally inappropriate behaviors.

The problem with this approach to categorize behaviors is that cultural behaviors are identified as *generally* situationally inappropriate, which connotes wrongness, thus suggesting that cultural behaviors are never appropriate in the school setting. Situational appropriateness is a matter of context (time, place, and circumstance); therefore, cultural behaviors cannot and must not be generalized as situationally inappropriate behaviors. So, to be clear, there are situations in school in which cultural behaviors can and should be considered appropriate. How, then, do we clarify this misunderstanding and apply situational appropriateness to the Pi chart in a culturally and linguistically responsive way?

Simple—we do not create a *situationally inappropriate behaviors* category in the first place. Instead, the Pi chart should have the following three categories: cultural behaviors, staff-managed (minor) behaviors, and office-managed (major) behaviors. Using this CLR version of the Pi chart, a school's diverse and inclusive CLR-PBIS leadership would then list behaviors that are cultural in the cultural behaviors column to clearly distinguish them from the cross-culturally unacceptable or "problem" behaviors that team members would categorize as either staff managed or office managed. Also, note the use of the term *cross-culturally unacceptable*. We use this as opposed to the term more prevalently used by educators with PBIS, *universally unacceptable*, because of how the term *universally* or *universal* often is defined from a dominant culture perspective. Moreover, the term *cross-culturally* explicitly signals that there is consensus that a particular behavior is unacceptable in any culture. By differentiating behaviors in this way, teachers, staff, and students will better understand the difference between cultural behaviors that are a matter of situational appropriateness and truly "problem" behaviors. Figure 5.2 (page 102) illustrates an example CLR Pi chart.

Apply the VABB Framework to Situationally Inappropriate Cultural Behaviors

The VABB framework applies in terms of responding to behaviors that are cultural and not cross-culturally unacceptable (problems). Before a teacher or staff member implements procedures to discourage problem behaviors or applies a hierarchy of consequences, he or she must first determine whether the behavior is cultural. If the teacher or

	Cultural Behaviors	Staff-Managed (Minor) Behaviors*	Office-Managed (Major) Behaviors*
Definition	These are cultural behaviors. They should never be conceptualized as "wrong" or "problematic." Teachers and staff should apply the VABB framework to students exhibiting these behaviors.	These behaviors are clearly not cultural. They should be identified as cross-culturally unacceptable, yet minor, by your CLR-PBIS team.	These behaviors are clearly not cultural. They should be identified as cross-culturally unacceptable, yet major, by your CLR-PBIS team.
Examples	• Talking with one another while working on an assignment (sociocentrism) • Shouting out answers (oral expressiveness) • Moving in seats while doing their work (kinesthetics)	• Cursing • Taking something without permission • Teasing other students against their will • Hitting another student	• Sexual harassment • Racial or xenophobic intimidation • Drug use or sale • Bullying • Physical abuse

*Note that the words *defiance*, *disrespect*, and *disruption* are not listed in this behavior Pi chart. This is because these behaviors are subjectively defined and, therefore, should *not* be included. In fact, we recommend that you never use any of these words—*defiant*, *disrespectful*, and *disruptive*—and even the word *insubordinate*.

FIGURE 5.2: Sample behavior Pi chart aligned with CLR.

Visit **go.SolutionTree.com/diversityandequity** for a free reproducible version of this figure.

staff member determines the behavior is cultural, then the next question to ask is whether the cultural behavior is the most situationally appropriate. If the behavior is appropriate for the context, then the teacher or staff member only needs to positively acknowledge the student. For example, a student is engaged in a group discussion and is verbally overlapping while on topic. This may be situationally appropriate for the context, and the teacher could affirm the student for his or her enthusiastic participation. But if the teacher determines that the student's behavior is *not* appropriate for the situation, then he or she could apply the VABB framework. The following scenario demonstrates how this works with a "blurting out" behavior.

The teacher validates and affirms the student's active participation in a group discussion by acknowledging his engagement and enthusiasm, saying something like, "I can tell how excited and engaged you are in the lesson by your spontaneous sharing." Now, here comes the hard part—without using deficit words, *such as* but *or* however, *the teacher then builds and bridges the student to the situationally appropriate behavior of turn-taking by asking him to cultureswitch because that was the prescribed discourse format (discussion protocol) for the group discussion. For example, the teacher might say, "We are using a turn-taking discussion format for this activity, so please bring that same energy and enthusiasm when it's your turn to share."*

In this example, and so many others similar to it, the teacher perceives the student's cultural behavior not as a problem but as a behavior that just might not be culturally appropriate for the situation. Moreover, this example illustrates an opportunity for the teacher to use the VABB framework to handle the situation in a culturally and linguistically responsive way.

Respond to Cross-Culturally Unacceptable Behaviors in a Culturally and Linguistically Responsive Way

What if you determine a student's behavior is not cultural but instead is cross-culturally unacceptable? Tier 1 PBIS practices call for teachers and staff to use positive and nonpunitive procedures for discouraging these unacceptable behaviors; this aligns with a CLR approach to responding to such behaviors. Where CLR and the typical tier 1 practices diverge is the use of a rigid hierarchy of consequences in response to students' "problem" behaviors. PBIS is not inherently culturally and linguistically responsive partly because of its inflexible systems (as noted in chapter 2, page 37). Teachers should respond to each incident of a cross-culturally unacceptable behavior—whether it is the first, second, or fifth occurrence—on an individual basis, helping the student take responsibility for her or his actions rather than merely comply with an externally imposed consequence in a lockstep manner. By responding to each incidence of unacceptable behavior as it occurs and eschewing a rigid approach, whereby each incidence is counted like a strike in baseball (which leads to removing the student from the learning environment on the third "strike"), the teacher or staff member would be handling incidences in a culturally and linguistically responsive manner because students who require multiple experiences to learn expected behaviors would be afforded these opportunities (Kozleski, 2010).

As noted in chapter 1 (page 9), the strategies put forth by Fay and Funk (1995) in their love and logic approach align well with CLR principles. This approach views students exhibiting universally unacceptable behaviors as opportunities to build students up so they become more capable of managing their behavioral choices. It focuses on developing students' internal control, versus their compliance with external control, through sharing decision making with them. Furthermore, Fay and Funk (1995) distinguish between punishments and consequences, noting that students regard both as the same if they perceive these consequences as externally enforced. This means if a teacher tells a student he or she has a consequence for exhibiting a universally (cross-culturally) unacceptable behavior, the student will still perceive it as a punishment, despite the teacher's calling it a *consequence*. To prevent this perception, Fay and Funk (1995) advocate engaging students in dialogue about their behavior and eliciting how they will take responsibility for their actions. We illustrate this with the following concrete example, which involves a minor cross-culturally unacceptable behavior.

One student tells a classmate she is ugly. The teacher overhears this and calmly yet assertively requests the student to come speak with her. Without judgment or accusation, she asks the student to explain what happened. The student then begins to explain that she called her classmate ugly because she was mad at her. The teacher first empathizes with her anger and then asks the student whether calling her classmate ugly was acceptable based on their classroom and school behavioral expectations. After the student acknowledges it was not acceptable, the teacher elicits from her how she can take responsibility for her actions. When the student offers a mutually agreeable solution (for example, stays in for recess to write an apology letter), the teacher accepts the agreement without any moralizing. Afterward, the teacher follows up to ensure the student followed the chosen consequence.

By handling disciplinary encounters like this one in a culturally and linguistically responsive way, teachers hold students accountable in a contextual manner that helps them develop internalized decision-making processes, which is far more effective than utilizing a preset hierarchy of predictable consequences to discourage "problem" behaviors. Moreover, it helps prevent teachers from thinking of the term *minor* as a noun and turning students' behavioral missteps into proverbial strikes against them. Treating students' behavioral miscues as strikes goes against PBIS's basis in *positive* interventions and supports, and it also echoes the punitive three-strikes laws that have contributed to racially inequitable mass incarceration. Of course, changing the way you respond to universally unacceptable behaviors takes a lot of practice, and students who are used to a compliance-based approach tied to a rigid continuum of procedures will need time to adjust.

But that was an example of a minor "problem" that is easily staff managed. What about those major cross-culturally unacceptable behaviors or those minor ones that persist? Are we saying that teachers should just talk those out with students and let them determine their own consequences? Let's take a step back for a moment and gain some perspective before answering. First, if your tier 1 practices are truly founded on CLR, then such incidents are far less likely to occur because the antecedents that may trigger those behaviors are less frequent. Furthermore, if you are using culturally and linguistically responsive trauma-informed practices, or healing-centered engagement as Shawn Ginwright (2018) conceptualizes these practices, then your classroom environment will be more welcoming and affirming, thus reducing the types of conditions that result in students exhibiting externalizing behaviors (major behaviors) that rise to the level of needing office management.

That being said, how can you manage such behaviors should they still arise? The core overlapping principles of CLR and love and logic still apply. Teachers should still respond to these occurrences calmly, yet firmly, with a clear message that they are not acceptable. For example, if an incident of sexual harassment should occur, a teacher or staff member must intervene and unequivocally message that such behavior does not align with the culturally congruent schoolwide behaviors. This is critical for ensuring all students, even those not directly involved, have a safe and welcoming environment. Because a diverse CLR-PBIS team collaboratively defined major "problem" or office-managed behaviors in advance, the next step would be to follow your school's office discipline referral procedures. The VABB framework and concept of situational appropriateness would not apply here because the student's behavior would not be considered cultural, and therefore need not and should not be validated or affirmed.

Even with behaviors considered cross-culturally unacceptable, though, teachers should still provide students an opportunity to learn from the occurrence, take responsibility, and atone for their actions. You might use restorative practices (addressed in chapter 3, page 53) to do this, but recall that this approach must also be implemented in a culturally and linguistically responsive manner to be effective with culturally and linguistically diverse students. Finally, teachers should make a collaborative effort to uncover why an unacceptable behavior occurred, or recurred, to ensure environmental conditions that promote cooperation with the schoolwide expectations are in place.

The Option of Referral

As previously noted, racial disproportionality in exclusionary discipline persists despite the implementation of PBIS based on standard fidelity measures. For example, Black students are vastly overrepresented in office discipline referrals, many of which are based on subjective reasons (Anyon et al., 2014; Bal, 2016; Eber et al., 2010; Parsons, 2018). By no means are we saying that teachers and other school staff should never use office discipline referrals as a response to "problem" behaviors. Conversely, teachers should use them in a strategic and equitable manner. There are times that a referral may be the most appropriate action for a teacher or staff member to take in response to a student's behavior. Therefore, how can you ensure that when you utilize an office discipline referral for behavioral support, you are doing so in a culturally and linguistically responsive manner? To help you respond to this question, refer to the decision tree in figure 5.3, which serves as a guide to help determine when an office discipline referral is appropriate and necessary.

Besides their inequitable use with students from underserved backgrounds, office discipline referrals can lose their impact on students when constantly overused and misused. Teachers who overuse or misuse office discipline referrals may lose standing and respect from some students, especially those who feel unfairly targeted. Moreover, this overuse and misuse can send students the message that the teacher does not care about them, does not have the skills to work with them, is scared of them, and even is prejudiced against them. Just threatening to use an office discipline referral can harm relationships with students. Additionally, when overused and misused, office discipline referrals can lose their impact on administrators and others who provide behavioral supports. Teachers who overuse or misuse office discipline referrals risk losing their administrators' and colleagues' respect and confidence in their ability to effectively manage students.

According to Dictionary.com (2021), to *refer* means to hand over for consideration, information, or decision. When referring a student to the office, teachers need to understand that they are literally handing over the responsibility of responding to a student's behavior to an administrator or other support professional. This may be appropriate if the school's CLR-PBIS leadership team considers a student's behavior major or if the teacher does not have the skills, knowledge, or confidence to handle the behavior. Optimally, though, teachers should do as much as they possibly can to avoid the use of office discipline referrals as a behavioral intervention because of the aforementioned drawbacks to their overuse and misuse.

Teachers should also be very clear about the purpose of office discipline referrals. All too often, teachers use them as punishments or scare tactics rather than processes for support. To ensure they use office discipline referrals in a just, culturally and linguistically responsive way, teachers must understand that the purpose of a referral is to have a process for getting extra behavioral support for a student who may need it (such as calming strategies or problem-solving skills) or for getting themselves the support they require (such as de-escalation techniques or CLR classroom management strategies). When teachers conceptualize office discipline referrals this way, they become less of a tool for removing students and more of a process for finding solutions, thus leading to more equitable outcomes.

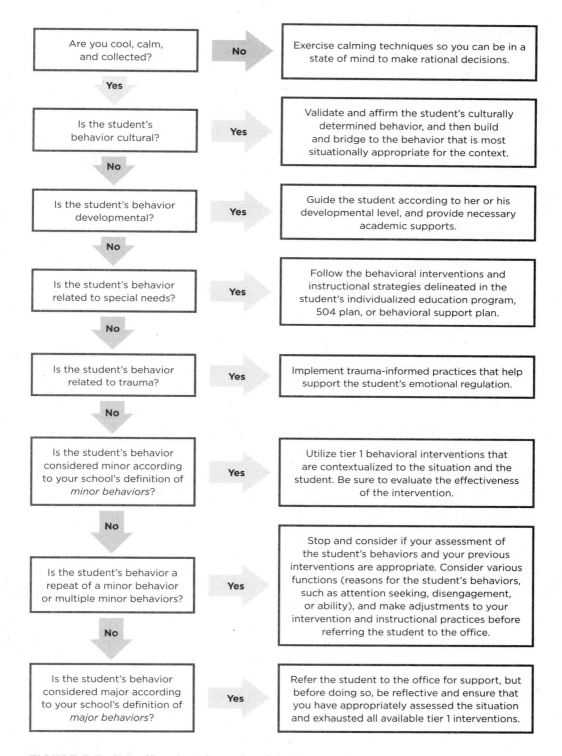

FIGURE 5.3: CLR office discipline referral decision tree.

*Visit **go.SolutionTree.com/diversityandequity** for a free reproducible version of this figure.*

Conclusion

In this chapter, we examined how educators must and can create situationally appropriate opportunities within the CLR-PBIS framework. Specifically, we focused on how to base several tier 1 practices on a solid CLR foundation. These practices include explicitly teaching students the schoolwide behavioral expectations, implementing procedures for encouraging cooperation with the schoolwide behavioral expectations, defining "problem" behaviors, and utilizing procedures for discouraging "problem" behaviors. Next, we will examine how to give students the language to be situationally appropriate within the PBIS framework.

CHAPTER 6

The Language of Situational Appropriateness Within PBIS

"SITUATIONAL APPROPRIATENESS IN ACTION"
DANIEL RUSSELL JR.

At CLAS, not only did we teach students about the concept of situational appropriateness, but we also created opportunities for them to practice being situationally appropriate both within and outside the school setting. This involved taking students on field trips where they were able to apply their knowledge of appropriateness for different situations. We visited parks, museums, and even the mall. One field trip stands out in my memory, though—a trip to Pepperdine University.

At Pepperdine University, we were going to attend a concert in the auditorium then visit the campus art museum. These different situations would provide students with the opportunity to practice various forms of situational appropriateness. What we did not know until the concert started was that it was a hip-hop concert. When the DJ dropped the beat and began playing the music, our students responded appropriately by getting up, dancing, and answering loudly to the DJ's calls. Meanwhile, students from other schools sat quiet and motionless while they watched our students enthusiastically engaging and furtively glanced at their teachers to gauge their reactions. Eventually, the students from the other schools caught on that it was not only OK to engage like our students, but it was situationally *appropriate. Even their teachers began to dance and rap. At one point, the DJ actually stopped the music to shout out our school for being the most engaged (and might I say, situationally appropriate) school audience he ever had.*

After the concert, we took our students outside for lunch and then to visit the art museum. As expected, they adjusted their behavior from the high energy and verve they showed at the hip-hop concert to what was more situationally appropriate in the quad area where we ate lunch and in the art museum. It was a marvel to observe the dexterity students exhibited in switching from one set of behavioral norms to another. It was clear that they had acquired the language of situational appropriateness.

In this chapter, we focus on how to give students the language to be situationally appropriate within PBIS. Specifically, we address concerns raised by teachers and teacher leaders regarding practical applications of CLR-aligned PBIS. Thus, we examine how the concept of situational appropriateness applies to different school contexts, such as hallway expectations, line procedures, and room-entering routines, to name a few.

First, as a model for how to give students the language of situational appropriateness, we describe our laboratory school's (CLAS) Ways of Being, Ways of Doing approach to teaching procedures and routines. Second, with that model as the backdrop, we review the concept of situational appropriateness in the context of specific school expectations for students. We do this by providing a method (the CLR formula) for clearly communicating behavioral expectations with a *general* CLR mindset and then digging deeper into having a *specific* mindset for situational appropriateness as it relates to CLR. Last, we provide questions and sentence frames educators can use with students to help them build the language of situational appropriateness while developing metacognitive awareness of situational appropriateness. The overarching point in this final chapter is that you can align many PBIS procedures and routines with CLR. So a key aspect of this chapter is to debunk the notion that authentic CLR and PBIS are incongruent. By focusing on the practicalities of what CLR-aligned PBIS looks like with students, we make the strongest case for why the alignment is important and necessary.

Ways of Being, Ways of Doing

It is critical to recall from chapter 5 (page 79) that you must examine how teachers and other staff teach schoolwide behavioral expectations compared to a culturally and linguistically responsive manner of teaching them. Culturally and linguistically responsive lessons are grounded in the linked concepts of situational appropriateness (validation and affirmation) and cultureswitching; use modeling and storytelling; utilize specific CLR engagement and instructional activities; and follow a three-step process for communicating the behavioral expectations (Sprick, 2009). At CLAS, we applied these guidelines and coupled them with shared behavioral expectations, creating what we called *ways of being* because they addressed how students and adults would aspire to conduct themselves and relate to one another. In conjunction with ways of being, we also addressed what we called *ways of doing*, which referred to the specific procedures and routines we encouraged students to follow, hence our approach's name, Ways of Being, Ways of Doing. As with any schoolwide behavioral expectations, we needed to explicitly teach students the routines and procedures following the same aforementioned lesson guidelines.

Sprick (2009) notes in his CHAMPS approach to proactive and positive classroom management that you can avoid a majority of "problem" behaviors by simply being very clear with students about how you expect them to perform certain tasks (for example, take a test, turn in homework, or enter the room). Sprick (2009) also recommends that teachers do this for every routine, procedure, or situation. Assuming students know the situationally appropriate ways of doing (when they have not been directly and clearly taught these expectations) leads to their ambiguous understanding of what teachers expect of them. This disconnect is exacerbated when students have to adjust to different teachers and staff (for example, when secondary students switch classes from period to period or elementary students have specials teachers whom they go to for art, music, or physical education).

Another aspect of the disconnect is that it often leads to a teacher's or staff member's cultural or linguistic misunderstanding of a student's behavior, which might result in a negative or punitive response to the student's behavior and an escalation in conflict between teacher and student. Therefore, teachers and support staff must invest time in explicitly teaching students the ways of doing for their classes and common areas in the school so they clearly understand what they are expected to do and how they are expected to do it. But if the adults in the building lack a mindset of cultural and linguistic responsiveness, even the clearest teaching of expectations can still have an undesired result for both teachers and students. Plainly put, you need more than just explicit teaching and clear understanding. Anyone teaching behavioral expectations must also understand the difference between cultural behaviors and cross-culturally unacceptable behaviors, CLR teaching strategies, and what it means to VABB students.

Clear Communication of Behavioral Expectations With a CLR Mindset

Clearly communicating expectations for the numerous and different routines, procedures, and circumstances means giving students the language to be situationally appropriate within CLR-aligned PBIS. Of course, clear communication is relative or in the eye of the beholder. To increase the likelihood of not only clarity but also student cooperation in regards to behavior expectations, we recommend the following CLR formula. This formula ($W_1 + H^2 + W_2$) is for communicating behavioral expectations in terms of situational appropriateness. W_1 stands for "what," H^2 stands for "how$_1$," and "how$_2$," and W_2 stands for "why." Students must know *what* they are doing, *how* they are expected to do it, and *why* they are doing it that way to ensure they have no uncertainty about what is the most appropriate behavior for any given situation at school.

W_1, or *What*

W_1, or *what*, refers to explicitly naming the procedure, routine, or instructional activity. By providing a specific name, you give students a mental anchor for situationally appropriate behaviors for that specific instructional activity or procedure. For example, if you are teaching a classroom procedure for turning in homework, you would explicitly tell your students the procedure's name, *Homework Turn-In Procedure*. As another example, you might want students to have a group discussion about a question you posed, and you tell them this instructional activity is called *Think-Pair-Share*. Overtly telling students what they will be doing and expressly naming the procedure or activity helps establish the expectations if you are introducing a way of doing for the first time and activates their prior knowledge about the situationally appropriate behavior for the activity if it is a repeat occurrence.

H^2, or *How*

H^2, or *how*, comes next and refers to two *how* questions.

1. How are students expected to perform the procedure or instructional activity?
2. How are students expected to behave in a manner appropriate for this particular situation?

Answering the first question clarifies for students the steps for a procedure or activity, whereas answering the second question addresses how you expect students to behave in a situationally appropriate manner during the particular procedure or activity. For example, you might have students working in small groups on a project. For H_1, you describe the steps they need to take to complete the project (for example, a checklist of tasks). Then for H_2, you explain what situationally appropriate cultural behaviors would look like and sound like for small-group work (for example, cooperation, voice level, and personal accountability).

Though there are various methods for communicating H_1 and H_2, Sprick's (2009) mnemonic acronym and method, CHAMPS, is an example of an effective tool (see chapter 1, pages 25 and 27). Whether you use CHAMPS or another strategy to help remind you to be explicitly clear with your students about the H_1 and H_2, you must frame descriptions of expected behaviors in terms of situational appropriateness around cultural behaviors and the opportunity to practice cultureswitching. Recall that this is essential for first validating and affirming underserved students' cultural behaviors, and then building and bridging them to school cultural behaviors that have been institutionalized as "normal" or "formal" (in a deficit way) in relation to students' home cultural and linguistic behaviors.

W_2, or *Why*

Finally, W_2 in the CLR formula refers to explaining to students *why* they are doing a procedure or activity in a certain way. When learners receive a rationale for doing something, it increases their engagement in doing it, especially if the reason given is relevant to them as a learner (Ambrose, Bridges, DiPietro, Lovett, & Norman, 2010; Mayer, 2011). This provision of the why for any procedure or instructional activity extends to relating the reason to cultural and school behaviors as well.

For many underserved students, field dependence (the need for relevance) is a deep cultural behavior that teachers must address in order to increase student engagement because context matters and is highly valued. Therefore, teachers need to be clear with students about the cultural purpose of a way of doing. This means letting them know whether the purpose is to validate and affirm a cultural behavior or build and bridge to a school cultural behavior. For example, if students are participating in a CLR discussion protocol called Musical Shares, you would tell them they are doing the activity to help those who need to process information through social interaction (the cultural behavior of sociocentrism) and movement (the cultural behavior of kinesthetics). Of course, unless you have front-loaded these terms, you might use more student-friendly terminology such as *learn better through talking with classmates* for *sociocentrism* and *learn better when you move* for *kinesthetics*. Alternatively, if you are having students work on a task independently, you might tell them that the activity is for practicing the school cultural behaviors of working autonomously (by yourself) and without movement, or what we call *stillness*.

Now, let's put the $W_1 + H^2 + W_2$ formula into action. Figure 6.1 (page 114) gives students the language of situational appropriateness in several different scripted scenarios. These various scripted scenarios demonstrate the CLR formula $W_1 + H^2 + W_2$ for clearly giving students the language of situational appropriateness. However you do it, remember the key takeaway is that students need explicit instruction on the ways of doing (for example, procedures, routines, and instructional activities). This helps develop students' metacognitive understanding of what it means to be situationally appropriate and to practice cultureswitching.

Also, be sure to increase student agency by involving students in the process of creating your class's and school's ways of doing rather than just telling them how to behave in situationally appropriate ways. When students feel like they have a voice in how things are done, like with teacher and school or district decisions, it increases the likelihood of them feeling empowered and choosing to cooperate, and not merely comply, with the expectations.

The scripted scenarios in figure 6.1 do not include the aspect of student agency, but they could be adapted to do so by asking students to list appropriate and inappropriate behaviors for each situation. Also, a word of caution: students often tell us what we want to hear about behavioral expectations rather than what they truly believe about what is appropriate and inappropriate (Kohn, 2018). So take care to monitor for this situation and stop it when it occurs to ensure that situationally appropriate behaviors for any particular procedure or activity are authentically culturally and linguistically responsive to underserved students and not just reproductions of dominant culture norms.

Finally, note that the example scenarios might not apply to your context as written, so feel free to adjust them according to your students' grade and developmental levels, including secondary educators. It is essential that middle and high school students are authentically engaged in this process of student agency as well.

Lastly, we must emphasize an essential qualification regarding giving students the language of situational appropriateness. We previously explained that teachers must give students specific positive feedback, not only for exhibiting the schoolwide behavioral expectations but also for exhibiting cultural behaviors. We emphasized that students' cultural behaviors must be validated and affirmed via specific feedback. This underlying concept applies to giving students the language of situational appropriateness. Teachers should not only ask students to be situationally appropriate to school cultural behaviors, they should also ask them what cultural behaviors might be the most situationally appropriate. This means that situational appropriateness goes both ways, not just the school culture's way.

CLR Instructional Activity: Graffiti Talk	
W_1	"Students, we are going to be doing an activity called *Graffiti Talk*."
H^2	"This is how the activity works. I will post several questions on chart paper around the room. When I give the attention signal by saying, 'Time to . . . ,' you say, 'Move.' Then, move to a chart paper on which to write or draw your response to the question. When you finish responding to one question, move on to another chart paper and respond to the question there. As you do this activity, you can talk quietly (voice level 1) with your classmates, or you can work silently and independently.
	"When you have responded to each of your chosen questions (you can do them all or the ones you can do), return to your seat. If you are still up and hear me say, 'Bring it . . . ,' then you say, 'Back,' and return to your seat. When everyone is seated, we will review the questions as a class. If you need help during this activity, be sure to check with me or a classmate. Any questions about the behavioral expectations for this situation?"
W_2	"We are doing Graffiti Talk because it is great for those of us who need to learn through talking with others, cooperating with others, feeling connected to one another, and moving."

Instructional Activity: Lecture	
W_1	"Students, I am going to provide a brief lecture about a topic."
H^2	"This is how the activity works. I will spend the next eight to ten minutes discussing the topic while sharing a supporting multimedia presentation. While I am doing so, I expect you to silently and independently take notes in your notebook for this course. You won't need to move for this activity, but if you need to get a tissue for your nose or get a drink of water, please do so as quietly as possible. If you have a question while I am lecturing, raise your hand, and I will call on you when I have a moment. These are the behavioral expectations for this activity that are the most situationally appropriate at this time. Questions?"
W_2	"We are doing the activity this way to give you an opportunity to practice working independently and silently."
Procedure: Walking in the Hallway While Other Classes Are in Session	
W_1	"Students, let's talk about our hallway procedure for when other classes are in session."
H^2	"When we walk in the hallway, such as when we go to the library, and other classes are in session, these are the situationally appropriate behavioral expectations. First, we will either be silent (voice level 0) or talk very quietly (voice level 1). Next, we will walk in a single-file line on the right-hand side of the hallway. We will also keep our hands to ourselves and not run or play. Any questions about how to be situationally appropriate?"
W_2	"We are going to behave this way in the hallway so we don't accidentally disturb other classes. We want to try to stay to the right side just in case another class might be coming down the hallway at the same time. Finally, we want to practice our schoolwide expectation of mutual respect."
Procedure: Walking in the Hallway at the End of the Day	
W_1	"Students, let's talk about our hallway procedure for the end of the day."
H^2	"When we walk down the hallways at the end of the day, these are the situationally appropriate behavioral expectations. It is OK to talk with one another, as long as we keep moving toward our dismissal area. You don't need to walk in a single-file straight line, but please be sure to let others pass by if they need to. As always, be sure to practice our schoolwide expectations to the best of your ability."
W_2	"We are going to behave this way in the hallway because it is the end of the day, and there usually aren't any classes to disturb. Also, I know some of you won't see or talk to your friends until tomorrow, so it's important to socialize with them."

FIGURE 6.1: Examples of activities using the CLR formula.

*Visit **go.SolutionTree.com/diversityandequity** for a free reproducible version of this figure.*

Teachers should give all students, regardless of background, the language of situational appropriateness. Applying the language of situational appropriateness unidirectionally, only to school cultural behaviors, can inadvertently imply that school cultural behaviors are better, normal, or formal. Therefore, teachers must use the language of situational appropriateness multidirectionally to prevent these misleading implications. Moreover, they must require *all* students to be situationally appropriate or to culture-switch, not just those from underserved groups.

The Mindset for Situational Appropriateness

Did you notice that the example scenarios in figure 6.1 (page 114) offered two different conceptualizations of situationally appropriate behavior for the hallway? Although this particular scenario is more relevant to elementary and maybe middle school, situational appropriateness for any given context or grade level will be relative. The *most* appropriate behavior for any given circumstance, whether it be in the school setting or elsewhere, is typically culturally determined. Moreover, what schools typically consider as most appropriate institutionally is defined based on the dominant culture's perspective (White middle class or Eurocentric). It's important to consider these dynamics when teaching or co-creating with students the CLR formula ($W_1 + H^2 + W_2$) for each procedure, routine, or instructional activity. Otherwise, you are in danger of unintentionally continuing to privilege only the dominant culture's perceptions of situational appropriateness or, worse, unknowingly falling into deficit thinking.

To help prevent perpetuating the dominant culture's notions of situational appropriateness and to build students' metacognitive awareness about appropriate behaviors, explain to students (or co-develop with them) different ways of being appropriate for any situation. For example, in the hallway scenario in figure 6.1 (page 114), situational appropriateness varies depending on the context. Sometimes, maintaining silent and straight lines may be the most appropriate, whereas other times, talking and walking in small clusters is most appropriate.

Figure 6.2 describes nine school scenarios, or contexts. Column 2 lists behavioral expectations for these contexts based on traditional school culture norms. Column 3 offers alternative ways students can demonstrate situationally appropriate behaviors that are culturally or linguistically congruent and also validating and affirming. You might consider reviewing the sixteen validating and affirming cultural behaviors in chapter 1 (pages 30–31) that are the focus of CLR.

These school scenarios or contexts are just a few examples of different situations in which students can exhibit situationally appropriate behaviors. Try to think of other scenarios or contexts and how students can show situational appropriateness in varying ways. Most important, remember that by engaging students in discussions about how to show situationally appropriate behaviors, you facilitate their metacognitive knowledge of how to assess different contexts for situational appropriateness and temporarily adapt their behaviors for these diverse contexts.

Context	Traditional School Cultural Behaviors	Validating and Affirming Cultural Behaviors
Paying attention during lectures or direct instruction	Sit silently and listen passively while taking notes.	Take notes while standing or sitting, depending on one's preference, and interjecting with connections or questions in an interactive way.
Working in the library	Be silent at all times.	Talk at a low voice level with peers about books.
Doing independent work	Sit still and work silently.	Sit or stand based on one's preference, taking movement breaks and calling for assistance as needed.
Having mealtimes in the cafeteria	Sit silently while eating.	Talk with peers at a voice level appropriate for the cafeteria setting (indoors or outdoors).
Talking in small groups	Take turns talking.	Include verbal overlap in conversations.
Responding during a lesson in class	Raise your hand to respond to or ask a question.	Spontaneously share a response by shouting out.
Going to the restroom	Use the restroom only during breaks, or ask for and receive permission to go to the restroom.	Go to the restroom as needed.
Following dress code policies	Do not wear hoodies or hats.	Co-construct dress-code policies with community members to reflect different cultural norms.
Riding on the bus for a school field trip	Sit silently.	Talk with peers at a voice level appropriate for the bus.

FIGURE 6.2: Situationally appropriate behaviors for traditional and culturally congruent behavioral expectations.

*Visit **go.SolutionTree.com/diversityandequity** for a free reproducible version of this figure.*

Situational Appropriateness Questions and Sentence Frames

Another way to provide students with the language of situational appropriateness is by offering questions and sentence frames. As you develop comfort and confidence with conceptualizing behaviors in the context of situational appropriateness, these questions and sentence frames can serve as scaffolds that help shift you away from deficit language. Remember that with the VABB framework, cultural behaviors are *validated* "to make legitimate that which the institution (school) and mainstream media have made illegitimate" and *affirmed* "to make positive that which the institution (school) and mainstream media have made negative" (Hollie, 2018, p. 28). Furthermore, teachers must *build* on cultural behaviors as assets to help *bridge* underserved students to school cultural behaviors through opportunities to practice situational appropriateness (Hollie, 2018).

Using the following questions and sentence frames can help replace deficit language in reference to students' cultural behaviors (which may just be situationally inappropriate) with validating and affirming language.

- What is the most situationally appropriate behavior at this time?
- How can you be culturally appropriate right now?
- Are you being situationally appropriate?
- If you were being situationally appropriate for this activity, what would it look and sound like?
- How could you cultureswitch so your behavior is situationally appropriate?
- Is this the appropriate time and place for that particular behavior?
- _____ is how to be situationally appropriate during _____.
- What does it look and sound like to be culturally appropriate during _____?
- You can be situationally appropriate right now by _____.
- In what way could you practice situational appropriateness while _____?

These are just a few examples of how you can frame behavioral expectations or build and bridge with students, giving them the language of situational appropriateness. Start by choosing a couple that you feel comfortable trying out right away; then slowly add others to your toolbox. Over time, you will find that both you and your students are speaking the language of situational appropriateness. Instead of seeing and responding to cultural behaviors as problems, you will view them as opportunities to validate and affirm students, while also building and bridging them to the school culture's ways of doing. Moreover, students will mutually develop an understanding of situational appropriateness that they can apply in a variety of contexts beyond school, and more important, they will not feel culturally misunderstood or unaccepted.

Conclusion

In this chapter, we examined what it takes to give students the language of situational appropriateness. This involves teaching the ways of doing (procedures, routines, and instructional activities) in a way that incorporates the concept of situational appropriateness. We introduced a CLR formula for this process ($W_1 + H^2 + W_2$) and looked at how to reconceptualize which behaviors are considered the most appropriate for diverse school situations to prevent the perpetuation of dominant cultural perceptions. We concluded with a sampling of questions and sentence frames to assist you in framing behaviors with the language of situational appropriateness and cultureswitching.

You may use the reproducible questionnaire on page 120 to help you analyze your classroom's and school's ways of doing (tier 1 procedures and routines) for giving students the language of situational appropriateness.

The Language of Situational Appropriateness Questionnaire

4—Strongly Agree; 3—Agree; 2—Disagree; 1—Strongly Disagree				
Level: School	**4**	**3**	**2**	**1**
My school's schoolwide behavior matrix includes descriptions of expected behaviors for common areas that vary based on situational appropriateness (time and context).				
My school's schoolwide behavior matrix validates and affirms cultural behaviors while also building and bridging to school cultural behaviors.				
My school's PBIS framework includes a comprehensive range of procedures, routines, and activities contextualized with the concept of situational appropriateness.				
At my school, the language of situational appropriateness (for example, with sentence frames) is used schoolwide with all students.				
At my school, all students understand the concepts of situational appropriateness and cultureswitching.				
At my school, we provide students with numerous opportunities to practice cultureswitching for situational appropriateness.				
At my school, students are not disciplined for exhibiting cultural behaviors that may not be situationally appropriate.				
At my school, students have many opportunities for their cultural behaviors to be considered situationally appropriate.				
Level: Classroom	**4**	**3**	**2**	**1**
My classroom's behavior matrix includes descriptions of expected behaviors for common areas that vary based on situational appropriateness (time and context).				
My classroom's behavior matrix validates and affirms cultural behaviors while also building and bridging to school cultural behaviors.				
My classroom management plan includes a comprehensive range of procedures, routines, and instructional activities contextualized with the concept of situational appropriateness.				
I consistently use the language of situational appropriateness (for example, with sentence frames) with my students.				

My students understand the concepts of situational appropriateness and cultureswitching.				
I provide students with numerous opportunities to practice cultureswitching for situational appropriateness.				
My students are not disciplined for exhibiting cultural behaviors that may not be situationally appropriate.				
My students have many opportunities for their cultural behaviors to be considered situationally appropriate.				

FINAL THOUGHTS

A Change in Mindset to Enhance PBIS

We wrote the first draft of this book during the first nine months of the COVID-19 crisis and during the fallout after George Floyd's murder and the ensuing so-called racial justice reckoning in the United States in 2020. Regardless of how schools structured learning during the pandemic, teachers were facing unprecedented levels of stress, pressure, and urgency to ensure that learning was as optimal as it could be, given the circumstances.

We submitted the final draft for the text three weeks before the 2020 U.S. presidential election. These were turbulent times on multiple levels that have created an edge, a tension, and a burden on educators that we had not seen in all our years in education. It brought to mind what our mentor Noma LeMoine used to say all the time: "You just ain't lived long enough." It was her clever way of saying, "You ain't seen nothin' yet." And she was right.

Yet, in this almost dystopia-like world, most educators we worked with, virtually or in person, were still committed to and focused on being culturally and linguistically responsive to ensure equitable outcomes for their students. These dedicated and devoted educators knew that being culturally responsive was more critical now than it has ever been before, and they are willing to do whatever is necessary for significant change. The pandemic acted as an accelerant to issues that were already present pre-pandemic and have worsened since.

At the same time, the murders of George Floyd, Breonna Taylor, and others shone a light on deep-seated racial justice issues and magnified calls for crucial changes. The United States had been here so many times before. These turbulent times forced a thought that was not new but could not afford to go unaddressed any longer. The thought was we, the schools, need to do something different that has a positive impact on the lives of all students, particularly students of color.

In essence, this book provided a two-part pathway for aligning PBIS with CLR and represents doing something different. The first part of this "road map" focused on the *why* of aligning PBIS to CLR to deepen readers' understanding around not only the meaning of cultural responsiveness but also a particular brand of cultural responsiveness. A rationale for the inherent disconnects between PBIS and CLR allows for clarity to better understand where the agreements and disagreements are so schools can resolve these differences to strengthen implementation. This rationale establishes the need for alignment. Making it plain, schools can do both CLR and PBIS. In reality, many schools have no choice but to do both because of the institutional mandate with PBIS.

The second part of the road map focused on the *how*. Just as you maintain your car, you must give CLR and PBIS a wheel alignment (to recall the analogy in chapter 4, page 66), followed by an assessment and finally a call to activate. Aligning, assessing, and activating are where the how begins. What rounds out the how is creating opportunities within PBIS that can teach situational appropriateness and give students those opportunities to practice so they can be adept at situational appropriateness. This is the goal for CLR for *all* students. In understanding the *why* and doing the *how*, you will enhance your PBIS, creating a win-win for the underserved.

APPENDIX

Abbreviations for Cultural and Linguistic Responsiveness

CLAS. . . . . Culture and Language Academy of Success

CLR. Cultural and linguistic responsiveness

IDEA. . . . . Individuals With Disabilities Education Act

OSEP. . . . . Office of Special Education Programs

PBIS . . . . Positive behavioral interventions and supports

PBS . . . . Positive behavioral supports

RTI . . . . .Response to intervention

SWPBIS . . Schoolwide positive behavioral interventions and supports

VABB. . . . . .Validate, affirm, build, and bridge

REFERENCES AND RESOURCES

Algozzine, R. F., Barrett, S., Eber, L., George, H., Horner, R. H., Lewis, T. J., et al. (2014). *PBIS tiered fidelity inventory*. Eugene, OR: OSEP Technical Assistance Center on Positive Behavioral Interventions and Supports.

Algozzine, B., Barrett, S., Eber, L., George, H., Horner, R., Lewis, T., et al. (2019). *School-wide PBIS tiered fidelity inventory, version 2.1*. Eugene, OR: OSEP Technical Assistance Center on Positive Behavioral Interventions and Supports. Accessed at https://assets-global.website-files .com/5d3725188825e071f1670246/60108a57b3fa685215c10927_SWPBIS%20Tiered%20 Fidelity%20Inventory%20(TFI).pdf on December 17, 2021.

Allen, R., & Steed, E. A. (2016). Culturally responsive pyramid model practices: Program-wide positive behavior support for young children. *Topics in Early Childhood Special Education*, *36*(3), 165–175.

Ambrose, S. A., Bridges, M. W., DiPietro, M., Lovett, M. C., & Norman, M. K. (2010). *How learning works: 7 research-based principles for smart teaching*. San Francisco: Jossey-Bass.

Anyon, Y., Jenson, J. M., Altschul, I., Farrar, J., McQueen, J., Greer, E., et al. (2014). The persistent effect of race and the promise of alternatives to suspension in school discipline outcomes. *Children and Youth Services Review*, *44*, 379–386.

Augustine, C. H., Engberg, J., Grimm, G. E., Lee, E., Wang, E. L., Christianson, K., et al. (2018). *Can restorative practices improve school climate and curb suspensions? An evaluation of the impact of restorative practices in a mid-sized urban school district*. Santa Monica, CA: RAND Corporation. Accessed at www.rand.org/pubs/research_reports/RR2840.html on February 9, 2021.

Bal, A. (2015, December). *Culturally responsive positive behavioral interventions and supports*. WCER Working Paper No. 2015-9. Accessed at https://wcer.wisc.edu/docs/working-papers /Working_Paper_No_2015_09.pdf on October 22, 2021.

Bal, A. (2016). From intervention to innovation: A cultural-historical approach to the racialization of school discipline. *Interchange*, *47*, 409–427.

Bal, A. (2018). Culturally responsive positive behavioral interventions and supports: A process-oriented framework for systemic transformation. *Review of Education, Pedagogy, and Cultural Studies*, *40*(2), 144–174.

Bal, A., Afacan, K., & Cakir, H. I. (2018). Culturally responsive school discipline: Implementing Learning Lab at a high school for systemic transformation. *American Educational Research Journal*, *55*(5), 1007–1050.

Bal, A., Thorius, K. K., & Kozleski, E. (2012). *Culturally responsive positive behavioral support matters*. Tempe, AZ: Equity Alliance at Arizona State University.

Banks, T., & Obiakor, F. E. (2015). Culturally responsive positive behavior supports: Considerations for practice. *Journal of Education and Training Studies, 3*(2), 83–90.

Barnum, M. (2019, January 4). *Major new study finds restorative justice led to safer schools, but hurt black students' test scores.* Accessed at www.chalkbeat.org/2019/1/4/21106465/major -new-study-finds-restorative-justice-led-to-safer-schools-but-hurt-black-students-test-scores on February 9, 2021.

Barrett, S. B., Bradshaw, C. P., & Lewis, T. (2008). Maryland statewide PBIS initiative: Systems, evaluation, and next steps. *Journal of Positive Behavior Interventions, 10*(2), 105–114.

Behavior Analyst Certification Board. (2021). *About behavior analysis.* Accessed at www.bacb.com /about-behavior-analysis on September 22, 2021.

Bekhor, J., Carter, J., Cohen, J., Jones, V., Pasht, J. B., & Slutsky, S. (Executive producers). (2019–present). *The redemption project with Van Jones* [TV series]. Los Angeles: Citizen Jones.

Besecker, M., & Thomas, A. (2020). *Student engagement online during school facilities closures: An analysis of L.A. Unified secondary schools' schoology activity from March 16 to May 22, 2020.* Los Angeles: Los Angeles Unified School District. Accessed at http://laschoolboard.org/sites /default/files/IAU%20Report%202020%200707%20-%20Student%20Engagement%20 Online%20During%20Closures.pdf on February 9, 2021.

Betters-Bubon, J., Brunner, T., & Kansteiner, A. (2016). Success for all? The role of the school counselor in creating and sustaining culturally responsive positive behavior interventions and supports programs. *The Professional Counselor, 6*(3), 263–277.

Blake, J. J., Butler, B. R., Lewis, C. W., & Darensbourg, A. (2011). Unmasking the inequitable discipline experiences of urban Black girls: Implications for urban educational stakeholders. *The Urban Review, 43*(1), 90–106.

Bohanon, H., Fenning, P., Carney, K. L., Minnis-Kim, M. J., Anderson-Harriss, S., Moroz, K. B., et al. (2006). Schoolwide application of positive behavior support in an urban high school: A case study. *Journal of Positive Behavior Interventions, 8*(3), 131–145.

Bohn, A. (2006). *A framework for understanding Ruby Payne.* Accessed at https://rethinkingschools .org/articles/a-framework-for-understanding-ruby-payne on November 3, 2021.

Bottiani, J. H., Bradshaw, C. P., & Gregory, A. (2018) Nudging the gap: Introduction to the special issue "Closing in on discipline disproportionality." *School Psychology Review, 47*(2), 109–117.

Boykin, A. W. (1983). The academic performance of Afro-American children. In J. Spence (Ed.), *Achievement and achievement motives: Psychological and sociological approaches* (pp. 323–371). Beverly Hills, CA: SAGE.

Bradshaw, C. P., Mitchell, M. M., & Leaf, P. J. (2010). Examining the effects of schoolwide positive behavioral interventions and supports on student outcomes: Results from a randomized controlled effectiveness trial in elementary schools. *Journal of Positive Behavior Interventions, 12*(3), 133–148.

Bradshaw, C. P., Reinke, W. M., Brown, L., Bevans, K. B., & Leaf, P. J. (2008). Implementation of school-wide positive behavioral interventions and supports (PBIS) in elementary schools: Observations from a randomized trial. *Education and Treatment of Children, 31*(1), 1–26.

Browder, A. T. (1992). *Nile Valley contributions to civilization.* Washington, D.C: Institute of Karmic Guidance.

Bridgestone Tire. (n.d.). *Tire alignment: What you need to know.* Accessed at www.bridgestonetire .com/tread-and-trend/drivers-ed/tire-alignment# on March 23, 2021.

Brummer, J. (2016, February 28). *5 reasons implementation of restorative practices fails in schools* [Blog post]. Accessed at www.joebrummer.com/2016/02/28/5-reasons-implementation-of -restorative-practices-fails-in-schools on February 9, 2021.

Buffum, A., Mattos, M., & Malone, J. (2018). *Taking action: A handbook for RTI at Work.* Bloomington, IN: Solution Tree Press.

Caldarella, P., Shatzer, R. H., Gray, K. M., Young, K. R., & Young, E. L. (2011). The effects of school-wide positive behavior support on middle school climate and student outcomes. *Research in Middle Level Education, 35*(4), 1–14.

Canter, L. (2010). *Assertive discipline: Positive behavior management for today's classroom* (4th ed.). Bloomington, IN: Solution Tree Press.

Canter, L., & Canter, M. (1976). *Assertive discipline: A take-charge approach for today's educator.* Seal Beach, CA: Canter and Associates.

Canter, L., & Canter, M. (1992). *Lee Canter's assertive discipline: Positive behavior management for today's classroom.* Santa Monica, CA: Lee Canter & Associates.

Castillo, J. (2014). Tolerance in schools for Latino students: Dismantling the school-to-prison pipeline. *Harvard Journal of Hispanic Policy, 26,* 43–58.

Castlebay Lane Charter Elementary School. (n.d.). *Restorative justice & social emotional learning at Castlebay.* Accessed at www.castlebaylanecharter.com/apps/pages/index.jsp?uREC_ID =1069281&type=d&pREC_ID=1362667 on November 3, 2021.

Center on PBIS. (2021a). *Assessments.* Accessed at www.pbis.org/resource-type/assessments on September 15, 2019.

Center on PBIS. (2021b). *Getting started.* Accessed at www.pbis.org/pbis/getting-started on September 15, 2019.

Center on PBIS. (2021c). *Tier 1.* Accessed at www.pbis.org/pbis/tier-1 on September 15, 2019.

Center on PBIS. (2021d). *Tier 2.* Accessed at www.pbis.org/pbis/tier-2 on September 15, 2019.

Center on PBIS. (2021e). *Tier 3.* Accessed at www.pbis.org/pbis/tier-3 on September 15, 2019.

Center on PBIS. (2021f). *Tiered framework.* Accessed at www.pbis.org/pbis/tiered-framework on September 15, 2019.

Charles, C. M. (2014). *Building classroom discipline* (11th ed.). Boston: Pearson.

Chugh, D. (2018). *The person you mean to be: How good people fight bias.* New York: HarperCollins.

Collado, W., Hollie, S., Isiah, R., Jackson, Y., Muhammad, A., Reeves, D., et al. (2021). *Beyond conversations about race: A guide for discussions with students, teachers, and communities.* Bloomington, IN: Solution Tree Press.

Cramer, E. D., & Bennett, K. D. (2015). Implementing culturally responsive positive behavior interventions and supports in middle school classrooms. *Middle School Journal, 46*(3), 18–24.

Dancy, T. E., II (2014). (Un)doing hegemony in education: Disrupting school-to-prison pipelines for Black males. *Equity & Excellence in Education, 47*(4), 476–493.

Dean, C. B., Hubbell, E. R., Pitler, H., & Stone, B. (2012). *Classroom instruction that works: Research-based strategies for increasing student achievement* (2nd ed.). Alexandria, VA: Association for Supervision and Curriculum Development.

Delpit, L. (2006). *Other people's children: Cultural conflict in the classroom* (Rev. ed.). New York: New Press.

Delpit, L. (2012). *"Multiplication is for White people": Raising expectations for other people's children.* New York: The New Press.

Dreikurs, R., & Cassel, P. (1990). *Discipline without tears: What to do with children who misbehave* (2nd ed.). New York: Dutton.

Dweck, C. S. (2016). *Mindset: The new psychology of success* (Updated ed.). New York: Random House.

Eber, L., Upreti, G., & Rose, J. (2010). Addressing ethnic disproportionality in school discipline through positive behavior interventions and supports (PBIS). *Building Leadership, 17*(8), 1–11.

Emdin, C. (2017). *For White folks who teach in the hood . . . and the rest of y'all too: Reality pedagogy and urban education (race, education, and democracy)* (Reprint ed.). Boston: Beacon Press.

Esquivel, P., & Blume, H. (2020, July 16). L.A. Latino, Black students suffered deep disparities in online learning, records show. *Los Angeles Times.* Accessed at www.latimes.com/california/story/2020-07-16/latino-and-black-students-hard-hit-with-disparities-in-their-struggle-with-online-learning on February 9, 2021.

Fallon, L. M., & Mueller, M. R. (2018). Culturally responsive wraparound supports: Collaborating with families to promote students' behavior regulation across settings. *Contemporary School Psychology, 21*(3), 201–210.

Fay, J., & Fay, C. (2016). *Teaching with love and logic: Taking control of the classroom* (2nd ed.). Golden, CO: Love and Logic Institute.

Fay, J., & Funk, D. (1995). *Teaching with love and logic: Taking control of the classroom* (1st ed.). Golden, CO: Love and Logic Press.

Flora, S. R. (2000). Praise's magic reinforcement ratio: Five to one gets the job done. *The Behavior Analyst Today, 1*(4), 64–69.

Fullan, M. (1993). *Change forces: Probing the depths of educational reform.* London: Falmer Press.

Fullan, M. (1999). *Change forces: The sequel.* London: Falmer Press.

Gardner-Chloros, P. (2009). *Codeswitching.* Cambridge, UK: Cambridge University Press.

Gay, G. (2000). *Culturally responsive teaching: Theory, research, and practice.* New York: Teachers College Press.

Georgia Department of Education. (2018). *Positive behavioral interventions and supports of Georgia: Strategic plan 2014–2018.* Accessed at www.gadoe.org/Curriculum-Instruction-and-Assessment/Special-Education-Services/Documents/PBIS/2014-15/GaDOE%20PBIS%20Strategic%20Plan.pdf on May 10, 2020.

Ginsberg, M. G., & Wlodkowski, R. J. (2019). Intrinsic motivation as the foundation for culturally responsive social-emotional and academic learning in teacher education. *Teacher Education Quarterly, 46*(4), 53–66.

Ginwright, S. (2018, May 31). *The future of healing: Shifting from trauma informed care to healing centered engagement* [Blog post]. Accessed at https://ginwright.medium.com/the-future-of-healing-shifting-from-trauma-informed-care-to-healing-centered-engagement-634f557ce69c on May 18, 2020.

Glasser, W. (1986). *Control theory in the classroom.* New York: HarperCollins.

Glasser, W. (1998a). *Choice theory: A new psychology of personal freedom.* New York: HarperCollins.

Glasser, W. (1998b). *The quality school: Managing students without coercion* (3rd ed.). New York: HarperCollins.

Goodman-Scott, E., Hays, D. G., & Cholewa, B. E. (2018). "It takes a village": A case study of positive behavioral interventions and supports implementation in an exemplary urban middle school. *Urban Review, 50*(1), 97–122.

Gorski, P. (n.d.). *Becoming a threat to educational inequity: The equity literacy approach* [Slideware presentation]. Accessed at www.edequityvt.org/wp-content/uploads/2020/02/Becoming-a-Threat-to-Educatinal-Equity.pdf on August 23, 2020.

Grace, J. E., & Nelson, S. L. (2019). "Tryin' to survive": Black male students' understandings of the role of race and racism in the school-to-prison pipeline. *Leadership and Policy in Schools, 18*(4), 664–680.

Greflund, S., McIntosh, K., Mercer, S. H., & May, S. L. (2014). Examining disproportionality in school discipline for Aboriginal students in schools implementing PBIS. *Canadian Journal of School Psychology, 29*(3), 213–235.

Guskey, T. R., & Huberman, M. (Eds.). (1995). *Professional development in education: New paradigms and practices.* New York: Teachers College Press.

Hall, G. E., & Hord, S. M. (2019). *Implementing change: Patterns, principles, and potholes* (5th ed.). Hoboken, NJ: Pearson.

Hammond, Z. (2015). *Culturally responsive teaching and the brain: Promoting authentic engagement and rigor among culturally and linguistically diverse students.* Thousand Oaks, CA: Corwin.

Hattie, J. (2012). *Visible learning for teachers: Maximizing impact on learning.* New York: Routledge.

Hawaiian Convention Center Blog. (2012, February 9). *Kupono: To be forthright, honest, and fair in your relationships with others* [Blog post]. Accessed at https://blog.hawaiiconvention.com/why-hawaii/kupono-to-be-forthright-honest-and-fair-in-your-relationships-with-others on March 5, 2021.

Hollie, S. (2015). *Strategies for culturally and linguistically responsive teaching and learning.* Huntington Beach, CA: Shell Education.

Hollie, S. (2018). *Culturally and linguistically responsive teaching and learning: Classroom practices for student success* (2nd ed.). Huntington Beach, CA: Shell Education.

Hollie, S. (2019a). Branding culturally relevant teaching: A call for remixes. *Teacher Education Quarterly, 46*(4), 31–52.

Hollie, S. (2019b). *Common cultural behaviors.* The Center for Culturally Responsive Teaching and Learning. Accessed at https://workdrive.zohoexternal.com/external/8OOPBDQFPPC-JBvLn on October 22, 2021.

Hunsaker, M. R. (2018, December 19). *External incentives DECREASE intrinsic motivation: Implications for classroom management* [Blog post]. Accessed at https://whyhaventtheydonethatyet.wordpress.com/2018/12/19/external-incentives-decrease-intrinsic-motivation-implications-for-classroom-management on 2021 January 4, 2021.

Individuals With Disabilities Education Improvement Act of 2004, Pub. L. No. 108-446 § 300.115 (2004).

International Institute for Restorative Practices. (n.d.). *Defining restorative: History.* Accessed at www.iirp.edu/defining-restorative/history#:~:text=In%20the%20modern%20context,%20 restorative,spree%20and%20agree%20to%20restitution on March 11, 2021.

Johnson, A. D., Anhalt, K., & Cowan, R. J. (2018). Culturally responsive school-wide positive behavior interventions and supports: A practical approach to addressing disciplinary disproportionality with African-American students. *Multicultural Learning and Teaching, 13*(2), 1–12.

Jones, F. H. (1979). The gentle art of classroom discipline. *National Elementary Principal, 58*(4), 26–32.

Kagan, S. (2002). What is win-win discipline? *Kagan Online Magazine, 1*(15). Accessed at www.kaganonline.com/free_articles/dr_spencer_kagan/301/What-is-Win-Win-Discipline on February 9, 2021.

Kagan, S. (2019). *Cooperative learning* (6th ed.). San Juan Capistrano, CA: Kagan Cooperative Learning.

Kagan, S., & Kagan, M. (2009). *Kagan cooperative learning.* San Clemente, CA: Kagan Publishing.

Kagan, S., Kyle, P., & Scott, S. (2004). *Win-win discipline: Strategies for all discipline problems.* San Clemente, CA: Kagan Publishing.

Kaplan, R. B., & Grabe, W. (2002). A modern history of written discourse analysis. *Journal of Second Language Writing, 11*(3), 191–223. Accessed at https://doi.org/10.1016/s1060-3743 (02)00085-1 on February 10, 2021.

Kaufman, J. S., Jaser, S. S., Vaughan, E. L., Reynolds, J. S., Di Donato, J., Bernard, S. N., et al. (2010). Patterns in office referral data by grade, race/ethnicity and gender. *Journal of Positive Behavior Interventions, 12*(1), 44–54.

Kidde, J. (2016, February 9). *Outcomes associated with restorative approaches in schools.* Accessed at https://livingjusticepress.org/rj-in-school on February 9, 2021.

Klingner, J. K., Artiles, A. J., Kozleski, E., Harry, B., Zion, S., Tate, W., et al. (2005). Addressing the disproportionate representation of culturally and linguistically diverse students in special education through culturally responsive educational systems. *Education Policy Analysis Archives, 13*(38), 1–43.

Kohn, A. (1996). *Beyond discipline: From compliance to community* (1st ed.). Alexandria, VA: Association for Supervision and Curriculum Development.

Kohn, A. (2006). *Beyond discipline: From compliance to community* (10th anniversary ed.). Alexandria, VA: Association for Supervision and Curriculum Development.

Kohn, A. (2018). *Punished by rewards: The trouble with gold stars, incentive plans, A's, praise, and other bribes* (25th anniversary ed.). Boston: Houghton Mifflin.

Kounin, J. S. (1977). *Discipline and group management in classrooms.* Huntington, NY: Krieger.

Kourea, L., Lo, Y., & Owens, T. L. (2016). Using parental input from Black families to increase cultural responsiveness for teaching SWPBS expectations. *Behavioral Disorders, 41*(4), 226–240.

Kozleski, E. B.(2010). *Culturally responsive teaching matters!* Tempe, AZ: Equity Alliance at Arizona State University.

Lanehart, S. (Ed.). (2015). *The Oxford handbook of African American language.* New York: Oxford University Press.

LeVan, K. S., & King, M. E. (2016, November 14). Teaching students how to manage feedback. *Faculty Focus*. Accessed at www.facultyfocus.com/articles/teaching-and-learning/teaching-students-manage-feedback on March 2, 2021.

Leverson, M., Smith, K., McIntosh, K., Rose, J., & Pinkelman, S. (2019). *PBIS cultural responsiveness field guide: Resources for trainers and coaches*. Eugene, OR: Center on Positive Behavioral Interventions and Supports.

Mallett, C. A. (2016). The school-to-prison pipeline: A critical review of the punitive paradigm shift. *Child & Adolescent Social Work Journal, 33*(1), 15–24.

Marshall, M. (2007). *Discipline without stress, punishments, or rewards: How teachers and parents promote responsibility and learning* (2nd ed.). Los Alamitos, CA: Piper Press.

Marzano, R. J. (2003). *Classroom management that works: Research-based strategies for every teacher*. Alexandria, VA: Association for Supervision and Curriculum Development.

Marzano, R. J., Pickering, D. J., & Pollock, J. E. (2001). *Classroom instruction that works: Research-based strategies for increasing student achievement* (1st ed.). Alexandria, VA: Association for Supervision and Curriculum Development.

Mayer, R. E. (2011). *Applying the science of learning*. Boston: Pearson.

McCold, P. (1999, August 7). *Restorative justice practice: The state of the field 1999*. Accessed at www.iirp.edu/news/restorative-justice-practice-the-state-of-the-field-1999 on February 9, 2021.

McGoey, K. E., Munro, A. B., McCobin, A., & Miller, A. (2016). Implementation of culturally relevant school-wide positive behavior support. *School Psychology Forum, 10*(2), 134–141.

McIntosh, K., Moniz, C., Craft, C. B., Golby, R., & Steinwand-Deschambeault, T. (2014). Implementing school-wide positive behavioural interventions and supports to better meet the needs of Indigenous students. *Canadian Journal of School Psychology, 29*(3), 236–257.

McLeod, S. (2018). What is operant conditioning and how does it work? *Simply Psychology*. Accessed at www.simplypsychology.org/operant-conditioning.html on January 22, 2021.

Midwest PBIS Network. (2015). *Culturally responsive school-wide PBIS team self-assessment, version 3.0*. Accessed at www.midwestpbis.org/materials/special-topics/equity on April 12, 2021.

Missouri School-wide Positive Behavior Support. (2018). *Chapter 5: Encouraging expected behavior*. Accessed at http://pbismissouri.org/wp-content/uploads/2018/06/5.0-MO-SW-PBS-Tier-1-Workbook-Ch-5-Encouraging.pdf on February 10, 2021.

Moemeka, A. A. (1998). Communalism as a fundamental dimension of culture. *Journal of Communication, 48*(4), 118–141.

Molinsky, A. (2013). *Global dexterity: How to adapt your behavior across cultures without losing yourself in the process*. Boston: Harvard Business Review Press.

Monroe, C. R. (2005). Why are "bad boys" always Black? Causes of disproportionality in school discipline and recommendations for change. *Clearing House: A Journal of Educational Strategies, Issues and Ideas, 79*(1), 45–50.

Morales-James, C., Lopez, L., Wilkins, R., & Fergus, E. (2012). *Cultural adaptations when implementing RTI in urban settings*. Accessed at http://rtinetwork.org/component/content/article/12/494-cultural-adaptations on October 17, 2019.

Muhammad, A., & Hollie, S. (2012). *The will to lead, the skill to teach: Transforming schools at every level.* Bloomington, IN: Solution Tree Press.

Noltemeyer, A., Petrasek, M., Stine, K., Palmer, K., Meehan, C., & Jordan, E. (2018). Evaluating and celebrating PBIS success: Development and implementation of Ohio's PBIS recognition system. *Journal of Applied School Psychology, 34*(3), 215–241.

Northeast PBIS Network. (2020, July 6). *Mini module: Overview of PBIS: A deeper dive* [Video file]. Accessed at https://youtu.be/nRQsyt7qjEY on October 30, 2021.

Office of Special Education Programs Technical Assistance Center on Positive Behavioral Interventions and Supports. (2015). *Positive behavioral interventions and supports implementation blueprint: Part 1—Foundations and supporting information.* Eugene, OR: University of Oregon.

Orange, T., & Hollie, S. (2014). A model for educating African American students. In R. A. Fox & N. K. Buchanan (Eds.), *Proud to be different: Ethnocentric niche charter schools in America* (pp. 61–80). Lanham, MD: Rowman & Littlefield.

Orlowski, J. [Director]. (2020). *The social dilemma* [Film]. Boulder, CO: Exposure Labs.

Parsons, F. (2018). An intervention for the intervention: Integrating positive behavioral interventions and supports with culturally responsive practices. *Delta Kappa Gamma Bulletin, 83*(3), 52–57.

Partners for Dignity and Rights. (2021). *Improving school climate through Race to the Top: Including positive behavioral interventions and supports (PBIS) in state grant applications.* Accessed at https://dignityandrights.org/wp-content/uploads/2019/11/PBS_RacetotheTop_FactSheet.pdf on April 8, 2021.

Pavlina, S. (2014, June 12). *What is respect?* [Blog post]. Accessed at https://stevepavlina.com/blog/2014/06/what-is-respect on February 9, 2021.

Payne, R. K. (2019). *A framework for understanding poverty: A cognitive approach* (6th ed.). Highlands, TX: aha! Process.

Peachey, D. E. (1989). The Kitchener experiment. In M. Wright & B. Galaway (Eds.), *Mediation and criminal justice: Victims, offenders and community* (pp. 14–26). London: SAGE.

Quarles, B., & Butler, A. (2018). Toward a multivocal research agenda on school gentrification: A critical review of current literature. *Peabody Journal of Education, 93*(4), 450–464.

Refer. (2021). In *Dictionary.com.* Accessed at www.dictionary.com/browse/refer on June 14, 2021.

Reinke, W. M., Herman, K. C., & Stormont, M. (2013). Classroom-level positive behavior supports in schools implementing SW-PBIS: Identifying areas for enhancement. *Journal of Positive Behavior Interventions, 15*(1), 39–50.

Ritter, G. W. (2018). Reviewing the progress of school discipline reform. *Peabody Journal of Education, 93*(2), 133–138.

Sabey, C. V., Charlton, C., & Charlton, S. R. (2019). The "magic" positive-to-negative interaction ratio: Benefits, applications, cautions, and recommendations. *Journal of Emotional and Behavioral Disorders, 27*(2), 154–164.

Samuels, C. A. (2013, August 27). Tensions accompany growth of PBIS discipline model. *Education Week.* Accessed at www.edweek.org/ew/articles/2013/08/28/2pbis_ep.h33.html on February 21, 2021.

Santrock, J. W. (2014). *Essentials of lifespan development* (4th ed.). New York: McGraw-Hill.

Schlechty, P. C. (2011). *Engaging students: The next level of working on the work.* San Francisco: John Wiley and Sons.

Scott, D. (2018). Developing the prison-to-school pipeline: A paradigmatic shift in educational possibilities during an age of mass incarceration. *The Journal of Correctional Education, 68*(3), 41–52.

Skiba, R. J., & Losen, D. J. (2015). From reaction to prevention: Turning the page on school discipline. *American Educator, 39*(4), 4–11.

Skinner, B. F. (1971). *Beyond freedom and dignity.* New York: Knopf.

Sprick, R. (2009). *CHAMPS: A proactive and positive approach to classroom management* (2nd ed.). Eugene, OR: Pacific Northwest Publishing.

Sugai, G., & Horner, R. (2002). The evolution of discipline practices: School-wide positive behavior supports. *Child & Family Behavior Therapy, 24*(1–2), 23–50.

Sugai, G., O'Keeffe, B. V., & Fallon, L. M. (2012). A contextual consideration of culture and school-wide positive behavior support. *Journal of Positive Behavior Interventions, 14*(4), 197–208.

Sussman, R. W. (2014). *The myth of race: The troubling persistence of an unscientific idea.* Cambridge, MA: Harvard University Press.

Townsend, B. L. (2000). The disproportionate discipline of African-American learners: Reducing school suspensions and expulsions. *Exceptional Children, 66*(3), 381–391.

Tyre, A. D., & Feuerborn, L. L. (2017). The minority report: The concerns of staff opposed to schoolwide positive behavior interventions and supports in their schools. *Journal of Educational and Psychological Consultation, 27*(2), 145–172.

Umbreit, M. S., Coates, R. B., & Roberts, A. W. (2000). The impact of victim-offender mediation: A cross-national perspective. *Mediation Quarterly, 17*(3), 215–229.

Umbreit, M. S., & Greenwood, J. (2000). *Guidelines for victim-sensitive victim-offender mediation: Restorative justice through dialogue.* Washington, DC: U.S. Department of Justice Office for Victims of Crime. Accessed at www.ncjrs.gov/ovc_archives/reports/96517-gdlines_victims-sens/welcome.html on March 30, 2021.

U.S. Commission on Civil Rights. (2019). *Beyond suspensions: Examining school discipline policies and connections to the school-to-prison pipeline for students of color with disabilities (42 U.S.C 1975a).* Accessed at www.usccr.gov/pubs/2019/07-23-Beyond-Suspensions.pdf on January 8, 2019.

U.S. Department of Education Office for Civil Rights. (2018). *2015–16 civil rights data collection: School climate and safety.* Washington, DC: Author. Accessed at www2.ed.gov/about/offices/list/ocr/docs/school-climate-and-safety.pdf on February 9, 2021.

Utley, C. A., Kozleski, E. B., Smith, A., & Draper, I. L. (2002). Positive behavioral support: A proactive strategy for minimizing behavior problems in urban multicultural youth. *Journal of Positive Behavior Interventions, 4*(4), 196–207.

Valadez, C. M., Porras, D. A., & 'Ulu'ave, L. (2018). *Classroom pedagogy and standard English learners: A study of five third grade classrooms.* Los Angeles: University of California, Los Angeles.

Van der Valk, A. (2016, Spring). Questioning Payne. *Teaching Tolerance, 52.* Accessed at www.learningforjustice.org/magazine/spring-2016/questioning-payne on March 30, 2021.

Vincent, C. G., Sprague, J. R., CHiXapkaid, Tobin, T. J., & Gau, J. M. (2015). Effectiveness of schoolwide positive behavior interventions and supports in reducing racially inequitable disciplinary exclusion. In D. J. Losen (Ed.), *Closing the school discipline gap: Equitable remedies for excessive exclusion* (pp. 207–221). New York: Teachers College Press.

Vincent, C. G., & Tobin, T. J. (2011). The relationship between implementation of school-wide positive behavior support (SWPBS) and disciplinary exclusion of students from various ethnic backgrounds with and without disabilities. *Journal of Emotional and Behavioral Disorders, 19*(4), 217–232.

Wald, J., & Losen, D. J. (2003). Defining and redirecting a school-to-prison pipeline. *New Directions for Youth Development, 2003*(99), 9–15.

Walker, B. L. T. (2020). "Loud, proud, and love a crowd": Black girls and school discipline practices. *Middle School Journal, 51*(1), 12–18.

Whitford, D. K., Katsiyannis, A., & Counts, J. (2016). Discriminatory discipline: Trends and issues. *NASSP Bulletin, 100*(2), 117–135.

Wilson, A. N. (2015). A critique of sociocultural values in PBIS. *Behavior Analysis Practice, 8*(1), 92–94.

Wlodkowski, R. J., & Ginsberg, M. G. (1995). A framework for culturally responsive teaching. *Educational Leadership, 53*(1), 17–21.

INDEX

The Will to Lead, the Skill to Teach
Anthony Muhammad and Sharroky Hollie
In this book, the authors acknowledge both the structural and sociological issues that contribute to low-performing schools and offer multiple tools and strategies to assess and improve classroom management, increase literacy, establish academic vocabulary, and contribute to a healthier school culture.
BKF443

Beyond Conversations About Race
Washington Collado, Sharroky Hollie, Rosa Isiah, Yvette Jackson, Anthony Muhammad, Douglas Reeves, and Kenneth C. Williams
Written by a collective of brilliant authors, this essential work provokes respectful dialogue about race that catalyzes school-changing action. The book masterfully weaves together an array of scenarios, discussions, and challenging topics to help prepare all of us to do better in our schools and communities.
BKG035

Overcoming the Achievement Gap Trap
Anthony Muhammad
Ensure learning equality in every classroom. Investigate previous and current policies designed to help close the achievement gap. Explore strategies for adopting a new mindset that frees educators and students from negative academic performance expectations.
BKF618

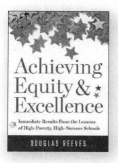

Achieving Equity & Excellence
Douglas Reeves
Achieve high performance for all in your school. In *Achieving Equity & Excellence*, Douglas Reeves shares the mindset of high-poverty, high-success schools and outlines how to follow their example to make dramatic improvements to student learning, behavior, and attendance in a single semester.
BKF928